A COMMUNICATIVE APPROACH TO CONFLICT, FORGIVENESS, AND RECONCILIATION

D1617360

A Communicative Approach to Conflict, Forgiveness, and Reconciliation: Reimagining Our Relationships synthesizes communication and psychology scholarship that focuses on rebuilding ourselves and our relationships when things go "wrong". It provides fresh insights into the burgeoning body of forgiveness research, with an emphasis on community application and reconciliation. Written by award winning scholars in forgiveness communication, the book makes forgiveness and reconciliation research accessible to students in courses focused on personal relationships, conflict, and family studies.

Douglas L. Kelley is Professor of Communication Studies and Lincoln Professor of Relationship Ethics at Arizona State University. His research and teaching focus on intimacy and love between relational partners and how they can respond humanely to hurt and struggle. He is recipient of the 2017 Bernard Brommel Award for Family Communication and author and co-author of five books, including *Communicating Forgiveness* (2008), *Marital Communication* (2012), *Moral Talk Across the Lifespan: Creating Good Relationships* (2015), and *Just Relationships: Living Out Social Justice* (2017).

Vincent R. Waldron is Professor of Communication Studies and Lincoln Professor of Relationship Ethics at Arizona State University. He researches communication practices that make relationships satisfying, productive, and just. He is author and co-author of seven books, including *Communicating Forgiveness* (2008), *Communicating Emotion at Work* (2012), *Moral Talk Across the Lifespan: Creating Good Relationships* (2015), *The Middle Years of Marriage: Challenge, Change, and Growth (2017)*, and *Navigating Work Relationships (2017)*. His work has been funded by the National Institutes of Health, the State of Arizona, and the Bernard Osher Foundation.

Dayna N. Kloeber, MA is a doctoral student and teaching associate at Arizona State University's Hugh Downs School of Human Communication and a former fellow of Arizona State University's Family Communication Consortium. Dayna received top student paper awards from the National Communication Association and Western States Communication Association for her research on conditional forgiveness. Her work has appeared in *The Journal of Family Communication* and edited books such as *Communicating Interpersonal Conflict in Close Relationships* and *Marriage at Midlife: Counseling Strategies and Analytical Tools*. Dayna's role as a community advocate for forgiveness education led her to create the Forgiveness Tree Ceremony and together with Vince Waldron and Doug Kelley she founded Arizona State University's Forgiveness Tree Project.

A COMMUNICATIVE APPROACH TO CONFLICT, FORGIVENESS, AND RECONCILIATION

Reimagining Our Relationships

Douglas L. Kelley, Vincent R. Waldron, and Dayna N. Kloeber

Routledge
Taylor & Francis Group

NEW YORK AND LONDON

First published 2019
by Routledge
711 Third Avenue, New York, NY 10017

and by Routledge
2 Park Square, Milton Park, Abingdon, Oxon, OX14 4RN

Routledge is an imprint of the Taylor & Francis Group, an informa business

Library of Congress Cataloging-in-Publication Data
A catalog record for this book has been requested

ISBN: 978-1-138-05264-2 (hbk)
ISBN: 978-1-138-05266-6 (pbk)
ISBN: 978-1-315-16635-3 (ebk)

Typeset in Bembo and Stone Sans
by Florence Production Ltd, Stoodleigh, Devon, UK

CONTENTS

PREFACE[1]

Reimagining Our Relationships has emerged from 20 years of conversations, data collection, theorizing, community involvement, and practice. This journey began with a decade of research on forgiveness, culminating in the book *Communicating Forgiveness* (Waldron & Kelley, 2008[2]). This early work on forgiveness triggered subsequent writing and ponderings that explore relational morality (Waldron & Kelley, 2008, 2015, 2018), justice (Kelley, 2015, 2017), emotion (Waldron, 2012), intimacy (Kelley, 2012), resilience (Kelley, 2017; Waldron, 2017), and reconciliation (Kelley, 2012; Kelley, 2017; Kloeber, 2011; Kloeber & Waldron, 2017). These various interests became pathways leading us to broaden our thinking as we considered constructive responses to relationship struggle. Ultimately, this book was born out of the realization that various elements of the forgiveness process can serve as a broader template for relationship change, whether that change is developmental or thrust upon us unexpectedly. In particular, we have become intrigued by the idea and practice of relationship (re)imagination.

The first section of this book, *Part I: Reimagining the Relationships We Want*, examines imagination as a productive source of relationship change, when things go "wrong". This focus has been influenced by a number of personally significant happenings in the last decade that have piqued our interest in imagination and transformation. Some of these are reported at the end of *Chapter 1: Reimagining Our Relationships*. As you will see, we use "wrong", not so much in its moral sense (although we do that too), but rather to describe how we felt when change disrupted our lives. This, coupled with reimagination, guides our personal accounts. Vince tells of his own experience with unexpected change as he came to understand his youngest child's transition from Laura to Lucas. Dayna reconstructs the narrative of how she reimagined her relationship with her mom, including the concrete choices and missteps that were made after finding her mother overdosed on prescription pain meds. Doug's story follows his journey through counseling with his wife Ann, and the process of reimagining their relationship as they learn that nice is not necessarily loving, honoring not always respecting, and people don't always change in the ways that you think best or want.[3]

Together, our personal and academic journeys informed the structure and content of *Reimagining Our Relationships*. While we recognize and teach that not all relationships are safe and desired and, as such, may be deescalated or discontinued, the focus of the current tome is how to move forward in a turbulent relationship that is potentially desirable and safe. As such, *Chapter 2: Cultivating Relational Creativity* presents a definition of relationship reimagination that serves as a guide for the rest of the book. In this definition we emphasize language, meaning, and imagination as critical components of personal interactions intended to heal emotional responses from past trauma and create a positive future. We offer various metaphors and sources of imagination that enable us to engage one another in personal and relational transformation.

The second section of *Reimagining Our Relationships*, lays the foundation for moving forward in our relationships. *Part II: Imaginative Work: Preparing for Change* focuses on catalysts of change, emotional responses, and sense-making. A significant lesson from our work is that, as important as it is what happened to you, it is equally or more important what you do with it. In this sense, *Chapter 3: When Things Go "Wrong" Catalysts for Relational Change* covers types of events that precipitate change (relational transgressions, relational trauma, relational stressors) and, importantly, reframes hurt, pain, discomfort, and struggle as *catalysts* for change. In this chapter we offer what we hope to be creative communicative responses to adversity, such as using talk as a means of creating resilience, moral common ground, and shared stories of redemption.

A significant lesson that arises from our personal reimagination stories, as well as our work with community groups, is that understanding and shaping one's emotional experience is critical to healing past hurts and creating a positive future together. *Chapter 4: Emotional Response: Motivation for Relational Change* looks at the role of emotion in various relationship processes, with particular emphasis on our emotional responses to particularly challenging catalysts of change, such as moral transgression. Key to the chapter is a focus on emotion as a central aspect of relational (re)bonding and healing. To bring this point home we look at two relatively recent approaches to understanding and experiencing emotion in healthy ways – Emotionally Focused Therapy and emotional intelligence.

What to do with the emotional experience and the unexpected change that has been thrust upon us? *Chapter 5: Sense-making: Understanding Relational Change* explores how we interpret what is happening during relationship adversity. Here we examine how hurt orients us to reassess ourselves, our partners, and the relationship itself, pressing us to deal with resultant high levels of uncertainty. It turns out that certain relational tensions and types of attributions greatly influence this process. Finishing this chapter, we discuss self-forgiveness. Our students and community members have taught us that often individuals have difficulty moving on personally, and relationally, when they are mired in shame and unforgiveness.

Chapters 3, 4, and 5 create a foundation for making personal and relationship choices to move on toward a hopeful future. As such, they set up the final section of the book: *Part III: Remaking Our Relationships: Personal and Community Applications*. Forgiveness is uniquely positioned to begin the remaking process since it deals with moral hurt, emotional pain, and making sense of our disrupted lives. *Chapter 6: Forgiveness: Reimagining Our Response to Personal Pain* begins by recognizing various quandaries and concerns about forgiveness, including potential dark sides to forgiving. These aspects orient us to imagine a forgiveness that brings personal and relational healing. We overview various communication aspects of forgiveness, and offer a new forgiveness definition that focuses on the imaginative elements of this means of transformation.

If you have read our previous work, or work of other forgiveness scholars, you know that most of us are careful to distinguish forgiveness and reconciliation and, further, emphasize that you can forgive without reconciling and reconcile without forgiving. In *Chapter 7: Reconciliation: Imagining a New Future* we note that reconciliation can take various forms, but we spend most of our time unpacking the *Communicatively Charged Reconciliation* model, which consists of six communicatively based charges for reconciling, or exploring the possibility of reconciliation, with others. At the end of this process we tackle two questions that consistently have emerged from our data and our community discussions: Is it okay to put conditions on forgiveness/reconciliation, and what makes a good apology?

The book ends with reflections on our relationship work in the community. In *Chapter 8: Reimagined Relationships: Community Applications and Lessons*, we discuss how we have brought our forgiveness and reconciliation work to schools, community centers, an adult detention center, and faith-based organizations. Through this process we have learned some unique lessons as we applied our theoretical frameworks into these diverse contexts. A special aspect of this chapter is the *Forgiveness Tree Project (FTP)*. The FTP uses a tree metaphor to engage community groups in discussion about forgiveness, and provides a collaborative, ceremonial opportunity for members to reimagine the bonds they share. We have included details for how to run your own FTP in a detailed appendix.

Reimagining Our Relationships has emerged as a natural extension of our lives and our work. It is designed for use with both undergraduate and graduate students, offering new models, fresh theoretical insight, and practical application. The ideas embodied here have already brought new life to our relationships and classrooms. We can only imagine what they might do for yours.

Doug, Vince, and Dayna,
April 27, 2018

Notes

1   We regularly reference this book using its subtitle, *Reimagining Our Relationships.*
2   Currently out of print, we have occasionally borrowed and paraphrased from *Communicating Forgiveness.*
3   Except for when we are telling our own personal stories, names used in quotes and examples have been changed.

ACKNOWLEDGMENTS

A host of students and colleagues contributed to the research and community outreach projects upon which this book, particularly the final chapter, is grounded. Among them are Vanessa Lopez Traslaviña, who scoured the databases for recent research on forgiveness. Megan Farnworth was meticulous in reference checking, APA formatting, and indexing. Students in Vince's COM 492 (Research and Conference) class adapted some of our forgiveness concepts for use with younger audiences, particularly our first group of Boys and Girls Clubs students. Vince will always remember fondly this enthusiastic group of graduate and undergraduate students. Cindy Becker, Wiwianna Lachowska, and Keisha Harrison worked tirelessly to adapt and present our Forgiveness Tree Project curriculum to Boys and Girls Clubs fourth graders. Dayna sends a heartfelt thank you to fellow Hugh Downs doctoral students from ASU's Transformation Project who jumped in to help on a variety of Boys and Girls Club projects. Rob Razzante offered his insight to the curriculum team and was a dedicated field observer. Megan Towles was an energetic and creative small group facilitator at Boys and Girls Club. Kat Hanna joined the research team and provided invaluable analytic and writing assistance. Dayna also owes tremendous gratitude to Drs. Jess Alberts and Sarah Tracy for supporting this cross-campus partnership. We are deeply grateful for their dedication, ingenuity, and enthusiasm.

All three of us extend our gratitude to students who helped plan the first Forgiveness Tree Ceremonies, shared their thoughts about social science expressed as art, and volunteered their time for video interviews. These include Shelbi Kidd, Joe Pullen, Gabriela Recendez, and Kathi English. Bonnie Wentzel and Saint Ranson also graciously lent their equipment and expertise to our video production. We also owe gratitude to the over 150 community members who donated seed money that helped us conduct forgiveness tree ceremonies. Their generosity provided paper for tree trunks, roots, branches, and supported Dayna's salary for a short time. Most of all their faith in forgiveness – their ability to *imagine* The Forgiveness Tree Project – fueled us to keep reimagining. It still does to this day

A special thanks to all of the leaders who invited us into their communities, and to all of the participants who engaged us honestly and openly as we have sought how to *reimagine our relationships*. In particular, we are thankful for the leaders of Boys and Girls Clubs of the East Valley and Phoenix regions, who recognized that forgiveness could play such an important role in cultivating healthy relationships among youth. Tonia Smith and Vonn Magnin are particularly notable for their congenial support and youth-centered leader-ship. Likewise, Doug is especially thankful for his long-term relationship with the staff at Neighborhood Ministries, and for all they have taught him about imagining and creating a better future for all people. Also, to Doug's interfaith panel of local religious leaders – much thanks for challenging perspectives and discovering unity.

Once again, we are reminded that good, supportive, and wise colleagues make all the difference. Jonathan Pettigrew was generous in his research advice in support of the Boys and Girls Club project that features so prominently in the last chapter. Catalina Cayetano provided unparalleled leadership and management of the *Neighbor's Table* reconciliation project (it's only just begun!). And, special thanks from Doug to his co-authors – ours has been an extraordinary journey of dynamic thinking, varied community endeavors, and valued friendship.

PART 1

Reimagining the Relationships We Want

1

REIMAGINING OUR RELATIONSHIPS

Kayla: You remember the day you were released from prison and got to come home?

Wendy: I do. I remember how you smelled. It was vanilla. And I remember the relief of . . . our lives get to really start from this point forward.

Kayla: I do remember specifically when you came home and you wanted to apologize. That was a defining moment for us because I got to tell you what I always wanted to tell you which was that, you know, you can never make up for that time.

Wendy: I, uh, bawled for days after the conversation . . . Did you ever wish that I was different?

Kayla: Yeah, for sure. I can remember, you know, writing in diaries about how much I hated you because you chose drugs over me.

Wendy: Why did you decide to forgive me?

Kayla: When you finally decided to get clean, it was obvious you were sincere. And, you're my mom, and as my mom, I loved you. I wanted that relationship . . . I'm happy where we're at today. And, I think what we've got is awesome considering where we've been. So I'm excited to see what happens next.[1]

★

The forgiveness negotiated by Kayla and her mother allowed them to reimagine the future of what was once a badly frayed mother–daughter connection. Their story, and so many others we have heard in the ten years since we wrote our book *Communicating Forgiveness*, prompted us to look closely for other transformative relational practices. *Reimagining Our Relationships* reports the results of our search. You see, most of us fall into our relationships. That is, we are born into a family, make friends with someone we sit next to at school or work, or "fall" in love. Like many things in life, we often don't think deeply about our relationships until something goes wrong. Kayla didn't have the opportunity to choose her mother. She was simply born to a mom who loved her, but who was also in a deep battle with drugs. Beautifully and honestly Kayla teaches us that even though she can't be sure of the outcome, she can imagine, and be "excited to see what happens next".

Reimagining Our Relationships[2] offers a rather unique perspective on responding to relationship change and difficulty. Specifically, we explore how transitional events, such as relational transgressions, developmental challenges, and environmental mishaps, can be dealt with in healthy ways. We investigate various processes that have emerged in relationship, conflict, and forgiveness scholarship (e.g., emotion processing, sense-making, empathy, dialogue, justice-seeking, extending mercy), that provide insight into how we heal the past and move constructively forward after relational disruption. To this end, *Reimagining Our Relationships* helps readers assess how to respond to past relational hurt, how to assess the potential for a healthy future relationship, and how to move toward reconciliation, when appropriate, desired, and safe.

Reimagining Our Relationships emphasizes imagination as a central component of creating healthy relationship futures. In the following pages you will be introduced to such transformational processes as empathy, apology, sense-making, and reconciliation. A fascinating, robust finding from research with unhappy long-term romantic partners reveals that these relationships are remarkably unimaginative, with distressed couples typically exhibiting rigid, predictable patterns of behavior (Fincham, 2004; Gottman, 1994). Yet, even partners who are relatively healthy frequently find themselves falling into all-too-familiar patterns of thinking and acting that are unproductive and hurtful (Kelley, 2012b). Our hope in *Reimagining Our Relationships* is to free relational partners from nonproductive patterns of thinking and behaving, and open new possibilities for positive relational futures.

This first chapter begins by examining what happens "when things go wrong" in a relationship. We explore how partners engage relationship challenges by grappling with two central questions – one oriented toward the past, the other to the future. This opens a discussion of themes that emerge from forgiveness and reconciliation scholarship, both rich sources of insight regarding how personal relationships are damaged, healed, and ultimately reinvented. We follow this discussion with discoveries about imagination and the central role it plays in strengthening friendships, romantic relationships, and families. This first chapter finishes with our own personal stories of reimagining our relationship frames – the narratives that guide how we do relationships.

A final note, before we begin. Throughout the book we use the term *relational partner(s)* as distinct from *romantic partner(s)*. *Relational partner* is an all-encompassing means of referencing individuals in any type of personal relationship – friends, family, or romantics. And, although much research on relationship reconciliation and repair is focused on romantic partnerships, you will soon discover that our focus is much more comprehensive.

When Things Go Wrong

Relationships can be confounding, difficult, hard work. Whether we are "soul mates", cousins, best friends, siblings, romantic partners, parent-and-child, or even friends-with-benefits, we eventually run into times where we find ourselves hurt, disappointed, or betrayed – trying to determine whether there is too much damage, difference, and emotional baggage to *make this relationship work.*

This may seem a rather dark, pessimistic view of relationships, but we believe that these relational challenges, as difficult and at times unfair as they seem, can create healthier people and, as a result, healthier connections between those people. The very nature of close relationships is vulnerability and co-created experiences with one's relational partners. This inherent mutuality and interdependence inevitably leads, in most relationships, to some type of relationship hurt or difficulty (along with, we hope, joy and intimacy). This hurt may come from betrayal, at worst, and disappointment at best (Vangelisti, Young, Carpenter-Theune, & Alexander, 2005) – the first situation being one in which important relational agreements have been violated (Metts, 1994), the latter representing unmet expectations we hold for our partners (Kelley & Burgoon, 1991). For instance, participants in one of our earlier studies reported needing to forgive their romantic partners for issues as diverse as sexual infidelity and forgetting a birthday (Waldron & Kelley, 2008). Wherever problems may fall upon this continuum, when adversity disrupts our relationships, it reorients the partners to consider two central questions:

- What do we do with the pain and hurt we are experiencing?
- How do we make choices that lead to a relationship future characterized by personal health for both partners, and relationship health that includes justice, connection, and a co-negotiated moral ethic?

Common responses to struggles with past pains and uncertain relational futures are to withdraw from other persons or situations, attempt to control them or, possibly, shut off oneself emotionally (Kelley, 2017). These strategies are typically used to shield oneself from past and future pain, and indeed may in some limited regard be effective in the short run. But, they are not sustainable choices for creating healthy, close relationships over time. More productive approaches can be mined from studies of forgiveness and reconciliation processes. As philosopher Hannah Arendt (1959) suggests, apart from forgiveness we are trapped in the irreversibility of the painful past and, without promise, we are lost in the unpredictability of the future.

Freedom From the Past: Themes From Research on Forgiveness

Interpersonal perspectives on forgiveness emphasize social aspects of this complex process. McCullough, Pargament, and Thoresen (2000) highlight the social nature of forgiveness when they state, "it is most comprehensive to think of forgiveness as a *psychosocial* construct", an "intraindividual, prosocial change toward a perceived transgressor that is situated within a specific interpersonal context" (p. 9). Therapeutically-based forgiveness models, such as those developed by Ted Hargrave (Hargrave, 1994; Hargrave & Sells, 1997), Everett Worthington (1998, 2001), and Robert Enright (Enright, Gassin, & Wu, 1992; Enright & the Human Development Study Group, 1991), provide insights into reimagining relationships, as they are designed for prescriptive use within specific inter-personal relationships (e.g., marriage and family). These models emphasize processes, such as "uncovering" one's own emotional response to a transgression (often by recalling the hurt), gaining insight and understanding, and recognizing decisional aspects of forgiveness ("Should I forgive?"). Maintaining forgiveness over time, by releasing oneself from negative affect that can potentially become an emotional prison, is also a consistent focus (Merolla, 2008).

Communication scholarship on forgiveness shares many features of therapeutic models. By its very nature, interpersonal communication-based research assumes a relationship between forgiver and forgiven and is oriented toward understanding the effect of forgiveness on relational, in addition to individual, outcomes (Kelley, 1998; Kelley & Waldron, 2005; Merolla & Zhang, 2011). Both communication and therapeutic models of forgiveness focus on aspects such as the emotional response to transgression, reframing, empathy, apology, compassion, and choosing to respond with mercy.

A prominent similarity between psychologically-based and communication-based models of forgiveness has been an emphasis on potential for reconciliation. As therapeutic models of forgiveness have been interested in teaching relation-ship partners to explore the possibilities of reconciliation, communication research has considered various outcomes of forgiveness episodes (Kelley, 1998; Kelley & Waldron, 2005; Merolla & Zhang, 2011), such as the relationship returning to normal, strengthening, weakening, changing type (e.g., from dating partners to friends), and terminating. These findings make evident that forgiveness reshapes relationships in myriad ways, only some of which resemble a "return to normal".

Somewhat unique to communication research on forgiveness is an emphasis on strategic communication practices used by non-therapeutic relationship partners, and the relationship effects of these strategies. How do people "normally" forgive one another, or seek forgiveness (e.g., apology), and what effect do these approaches have on relationships? A good example of communication work in this arena is Kloeber and Waldron's (2017) exploration of conditional forgiveness ("I'll forgive you if . . ."). In this study they identify the modes in which conditional forgiveness is expressed and explore the often-found link between conditional forgiveness and relationship decline (Kloeber & Waldron, 2017; Waldron & Kelley, 2005). Similarly, work by Merolla (2017) has focused on "the commonness of forgiveness style usage and determining the extent to which different forgiveness styles shape personal and relational well-being" (p. 237).

A number of interpersonal forgiveness themes guided us in creating a definition of relationship renewal that helps partners imaginatively gain freedom from past hurt while reimagining their current and future relationships. We highlight a sampling of these themes here (see Box 1.1), and present the full definition in *Chapter 2: Cultivating Relational Creativity*. Two themes central to reimagining past and future are negotiation and dialogue. Negotiating differences and engaging in rich dialogue enable individuals to work through relational disruption and renegotiate the terms of their relationship transition (e.g., does the relationship continue and, if so, how might relationship agreements be modified? Waldron & Kelley, 2008). These elements are consonant with research on strategies used to grant and seek forgiveness (Kelley & Waldron, 2005; Waldron & Kelley, 2005), especially the plethora of work on apology (Fehr, Gelfand, & Nag, 2010), as well

---

BOX 1.1 REIMAGINATION THEMES FROM FORGIVENESS RESEARCH

Dialogue – understanding and embracing differences.

Negotiation – establishing a shared moral ethic.

Communication Practices – discussion/explanation, nonverbal responsiveness and sincerity, apology, restitution, setting boundaries.

Emotional Expression and Management – emotional response, emotional intelligence, emotional connection.

Hurt – a type of emotional response, particularly related to relationship disruption and cycles of sense-making responses.

Empathic Response – connection, understanding, rehumanization.

Justice/Mercy – fairness, future, and well-being; dialectic of accountability and benevolence.

Sense-making – (re)interpreting the actions, motives, and identities of self and partner.

Healing – Letting go, regeneration, moving forward.

that focused on relationship processes such as setting boundaries (Docan-Morgan, 2014; Galvin, 2006) and renegotiating the moral ethic of the relationship (Kelley, 2012; Waldron & Kelley, 2008).

The expression and management of emotion has been of keen interest as researchers explore reactions to hurt and its impact on future relationship parameters (Waldron & Kelley, 2008). Key questions have included: How do emotional responses vary by kind of transgression (Guerrero & Cole, 2015)? How do individuals respond to hurtful acts committed by friends and lovers (Feeney, 2005; Vangelisti, 2009)? How do couples move on from negative emotion after marital infidelity (Gordon, Baucom, & Snyder, 2004, 2005)? Similarly, research on empathy has focused on both affective and cognitive characteristics with demonstrated links to essential relationship processes such as compassion, understanding, and mercy (Fehr et al., 2010; Murphy & Hampton, 1998; Worthington, 1998). Significantly, this type of work has generated questions regarding the role of mercy and justice in relationships, resulting in interesting exploration of atonement, restitution, and revenge (Kloeber, 2011; Waldron & Kelley, 2008; Yoshimura & Boon, 2018), aspects of justice that influence personal relationships (Kelley, 2015, 2017), and, more broadly, efforts that accentuate the moral aspect of personal relationships and emphasize how relational moral ethics are negotiated (Kelley, 2012; Waldron & Kelley, 2008; Waldron & Kelley, 2015).

Constructing a Positive Future: Themes From Research on Reconciliation

Reconciliation in personal relationships has been written about from a variety of perspectives and represented by the metaphors of maintenance, repair, conflict management, relationship recovery, and, of course, reconciliation. Whereas these terms typically share a common meaning regarding the continuance of an established relationship, there are notable distinctions. For instance, maintenance generally refers to attempts to "preserve ongoing relationships" and "sustain desired relational definitions" (Canary & Stafford, 1992, p. 243), without reference to a traumatic event or transgression. Likewise, those who study conflict management have often focused on styles and strategies used to resolve various types of problems and issues (Putnam, 2006), with less of an eye toward restoring a damaged relationship. Repair, on the other hand, has presumed some type of damage and the need for restoration or to be "fixed" (Merolla, 2017). In this same vein, researchers studying couples who have endured infidelity have referred to the process as one of recovery (Gordon et al., 2004) – much like a body recovers from illness.

In *Reimagining Our Relationships*, we have chosen to focus on the term *reconciliation* for a number of reasons. First, while the aforementioned terminology is certainly appropriate within certain contexts, we find it limiting in terms of reimagining one's relationships. For example, maintenance and repair are mechanistic metaphors that conjure images of preserving what is normative or returning something to its previous state. Regarding conflict management, our central concern is that "management" implies keeping things under control to maintain the status quo. In the same way, recovery is often associated with getting one's health "back to normal".

In contrast to these associations, reconciliation implies a reconnecting of relational partners. In fact, it has been argued that all communication is "re-conciliation" at some level (Kelley, 2017). In the broadest sense of the term, each time relational partners come together in a conciliatory or compatible manner (conciliate actually comes from Latin roots meaning to bring together or unite; Hoad, 1986) they experience a reconciliation. This reunion, of sorts, is characterized by a sharing of new events and experiences. In this way, reconciling always involves a certain amount of adaptation and co-creation. Part of our enthusiasm for reconciliation is that it is always about jointly reimagined relationships.

Reconciliation is ideologically and practically important for another reason – it has been a central theme in the social justice literature (Frey, 2009). Although steeped in a critical approach to viewing and responding to social groups (Frey & Palmer, 2017), social justice perspectives provide a fruitful means of exploring the realm of struggle in personal relationships. As Kelley (2017) suggests, "The essence of justice is creating spaces where relationship partners are able to embrace their full humanity" (p. xiv). Working from this perspective, reconciliation is more than simply relationship restoration. It is a process that encourages transformation, systemic change (e.g., adapting family structures), restoration of power balance and equity, renegotiation of relational values, reestablishment of the relationship moral ethic, and partners advocating for one another, showing mercy to one another, loving one another and, essentially, rehumanizing one another (Dempsey et al., 2011; Kelley, 2017).

It is also important to emphasize that reconciliation processes, reimagining and renegotiating one's relationship, may at times lead to relationship termination, or a significant change in relationship type or quality. Engaging in dialogue over past hurts or dreams for the future is a messy process that may lead to discovery of new information or emotional responses that forestall attempts to reunite (Waldron & Kelley, 2008). For example, attempts to reconcile divorced partners with children could take varied forms – complete separation from one another (if one parent has sole-custody); connected as parents, but no longer as lovers; co-parenting friendship; or, limited social media contact from the out-of-state, noncustodial parent. Additionally, reconciliation may take place both with, and without, forgiveness, although we argue that full reconciliation typically involves the forgiveness process. Think of sisters who forgive one another for hurtful statements made in their teens, and fully reunite, or, alternatively, harbor grudges over those hurtful statements while maintaining connection "for Mom's sake" or because "that's what sisters do".

As varied as forms of reconciliation may be (e.g., full, partial, for someone else's benefit, change in relationship type, with or without forgiveness), it is essential that *relational partners understand that they do not have to reconcile, even if they forgive one another.* As we contend throughout the book, *reconciliation should only take place when the relationship is appropriate, desired, and emotionally and physically safe for both partners.*

Imagining New Relational Futures

Forgiveness and reconciliation are dependent on imagination. Merolla (2017) makes this clear as he summarizes a reconciliation that took place between mother and son, Connie and Samuel, after years of difficulty regarding Samuel's homosexuality: "Connie and Samuel *reimagined* (italics ours) their past, present, and future and renegotiated their value systems to transcend their discord . . ." (p. 228). Likewise, Kayla and her mother, Wendy, whose dialogue introduces the beginning of this chapter, dealt with their past, present, and future by reimagining their painful history, the potentialities of their current interactions, their own identities, and their possible future together as daughter and mother. For Kayla, this undoubtedly meant rethinking whether her mother actually "chose drugs over me", while Wendy reimagined her own identity: "Can I be a better mom". Wendy engaged her imagination to apologize to Kayla for being gone during critical high school years, whereas that very same apology opened a window for Kayla to say what she had been imagining she would say ("you can never make up for that time"). Together, deciding to "get clean" and embracing the nature of their relationship ("you're my mom, and as my mom, I loved you") created imaginative space for a joint future together as mother and daughter ("our lives get to really start from this point forward").

The previous examples highlight key aspects of how relationship partners actually rebuild their relationships. Work by Feeney (2009) suggests that when individuals are hurt, it reorients the relationship partners to ask questions regarding their own identity ("Why does this type of thing keep happening to me?", "Am I loveable?") and the nature of the partner ("I don't know who you are any more", "Can I trust you?"). Likewise, Waldron and Kelley (2008) suggest that part of the forgiveness process is assessing one's own and one's partner's identity, and whether the relationship is still safe and desirable. This reorientation requires an openness to reimagining who we are, who our partner is, and together, what we might become.

Before we close this opening chapter with our own reimagination stories, we want to emphasize a central element that carries through *Reimagining Our Relationships* – (re)imagination is needed for hope. An example of how imagining a positive future is useful in creating hope and current happiness emerges from a study, by Honeycutt and Wiemann (1999), that found engaged couples were happier when they cultivated positive images of a joint future. Creating positive beliefs about one's relationship and its possibilities is essential to maintaining our relationships and overcoming relationship difficulties (Kelley, 2017). This simple principle was made all too evident by a former student. Macon found himself in a place, with his wife Jenna, unable to imagine a future where his needs were met. After two years of adventure, bouncing around the country, both working part time, Jenna had secured a challenging job. It didn't pay a lot, but she found meaning in her work for a struggling nonprofit. Macon, by contrast, felt lost in this transition. He floundered to find a role in this new stage of their relationship, and subsequently struggled to imagine a fulfilling future with Jenna. Unfortunately, he all too easily began to imagine an exciting future with a mutual friend, Sheila. Nine months later, Macon told Jenna he was leaving her, to travel with Sheila. As much as Jenna and friends asked him to reconsider, to dialogue, to reimagine possibilities, Macon refused, convinced the die was cast. He couldn't imagine his relationship with Jenna ever really changing.

As Macon's story illustrates, imagination and hope are necessary to overcome relationship difficulties (Waldron & Kelley, 2008). After relationship harm has taken place, reimagining and negotiating a shared relational moral ethic, and promising to work toward fulfillment of that ethic, can create some measure of hope for the future. The process of dialogue, itself, can be humanizing, helping to infuse a positive sense of possibility (Kelley, 2017) that may result in a new confidence in relational rules, reestablished accountability, and diminished defensiveness, guilt, and desire for revenge. With time, feelings of fairness, equity, trust, and closeness may also return.

When relational disruptions are engaged and processed, key questions raised by the catalyst event are productively explored – Why did this "wrong" happen to us? Who takes responsibility? How can things be made right? What does the future hold for this relationship? "What does it say about me, if I stay in a relationship with you?" The emotional response and cognitive uncertainty experienced during this relational transition are placed more firmly in the past and the groundwork for the relational future is laid. Ultimately, key communicative processes make it possible for wounded people to imagine a future in which their individual dignity is honored, and a new sense of relational justice prevails. Given these positive prospects, feelings of hostility and the desire for revenge may be replaced by hope and even positive regard for those who have participated in this trying process.

Reconsider Wendy and Kayla's reconciliation. Listen to Kayla's words to her mother, "I'm happy we're where we're at today. And, I think what we've got is awesome considering where we've been. So I'm excited to see what happens next" (White & Mullen, 2017). Kayla would never have chosen to go through all the pain she did with her mother. However, their ability to reimagine themselves and their relationship resulted in a positive, transformed, co-created mother–daughter bond. As stated by Pulitzer Prize nominated author, Frederick Buechner, we must "be good stewards of our pain". Kayla and Wendy have done just that. And we can, too, through *Reimagining Our Relationships*.

Reimagining Your Relationship Frame: Our Personal Stories

A significant aspect of *Reimagining Our Relationships* is creating a new relationship worldview, or relationship frame (Kelley, 2017). Relationship frames are essentially meta-narratives that guide how we interpret and engage the relationships of our lives. As we *reimagine our relationships*, we are doing more than simply learning a new skill or two, or gaining a new perspective on a specific action or event, as important as those things are. We are learning to rethink what relationships mean to us, and how we "do" those relationships. This involves seeing ourselves, our relationship partners, and our relationships with fresh eyes. As such, to begin this journey, we want to take a moment to share with you portions of each of our own *reimagination journeys*.

Vince: The Son I Always Had

Given the way things turned out, it is not surprising that when "Laura" was born, I thought she was a boy.

Our first born, Emily, was something of a miracle child, surviving a traumatic delivery and 50–50 prognosis of survival. So, when she was a thriving two-year-old girl, it was with awe and trepidation that I watched the beautiful, wrinkly face of our second baby emerge from Kathleen's body. For a second, or maybe two, I can't even explain why, I believed that I was seeing a male face, the face of our son. And as the anatomical truth came into view, I distinctly remember a tiny, fleeting feeling of loss. It was quickly extinguished, washed away by a sudden and joyful realization – Emily would have a sister to play with! As nurses bustled around the delivery room, I remember gazing at Kathleen, who was tired yet beaming. I smiled, fast-forwarding through the years as I imagined us parenting two strong daughters, sisters bonded for life by sibling affection and parental love.

Now, some 26 years later, I still wonder about that initial pang of loss. I really don't recall hoping that our second child might share my own gender. In fact, as the oldest of three sons, I found myself gobsmacked with wonder as we parented Emily – a deeply curious and observant child, joyful and loving, a verbal wizard at the age of 24 months. When I allowed myself to speculate about the gender of our new baby, I imagined "girl". But in the delivery room that night I must have grieved subconsciously at the realization that I would never have the chance to share with a son my own experience as a boy, a sibling, a man, a dad.

During the early years, the child I now know as Lucas showed little interest in traditionally masculine pursuits. Cheerful and wildly inventive, my youngest enacted her assigned identity by donning elaborate ball gowns and singing like a canary as the two sisters and their girlfriends staged elaborate, angst-filled, seemingly endless "plays" before audiences of bemused parents. Perhaps blinded by our own lack of imagination when it came to gender orientation, Kathleen and I were slow to notice that for Laura, the real masquerade was feeling like a boy but living as a girl.

Of course, there were signs, some of which seem obvious in retrospect. Lucas has always shared qualities with his mother, including a quick wit and razor-sharp intelligence. But as the years passed, our youngest bonded fiercely with me when it came to such activities as competitive sports, hiking, and fishing. Competing with girls first, then with boys, "Laura" was a scrappy, tough athlete – a kid who absolutely thrived on physical challenges and chafed at any limitation placed on female competitors. Barely 5 feet tall, our child insisted on competing with boys, even when the "boys" grew whiskers and soared over 6 feet in height. At school, the teachers reported our kid insisted on standing in the "boys line". At home, we noticed that our exuberant little girl child was becoming a depressed teenager, one who increasingly dressed and acted as an out-of-sorts teenage boy.

Although sometimes puzzled, Kathleen and I took great pride in our "tom boy", the kid who smashed gender barriers and showed such courage in the face of inevitable backlash from peers and adult rule makers. And when we realized that our child was showing signs of being attracted to women, we were so relieved. "We have a gay daughter!" That explained it. We just needed to reimagine our child's relational future, to offer our assurance and support until she grew more comfortable with her sexuality and the depression lifted.

But as the years passed, Lucas began to drop hints for his clueless parents. Luc helped us see that his identity could not be expressed in the role of daughter or by the name of Laura. "Remember, back in fourth grade," he explained, "when I would refuse to stand in the 'girl's line'? It wasn't that I wanted to be *with* the boys. I felt like I *was* a boy." That insight, that my child always viewed himself as a boy, fundamentally changed our relationship. It helped me to reimagine and reconstruct the story of our past, to see it through the eyes of my courageous kid. Luc had negotiated the difficult terrain of childhood and adolescence while carrying a crushing burden, an identity that he could not express to us, to his friends, not even to himself. Despite loving him with all of my heart, I had failed to recognize what I knew in the delivery room all those years ago.

Lucas was in college before I became, officially, the father of a son. It was only then that he felt comfortable enough to choose a more appropriate name, invite his family to meet the "real" Lucas, and change his appearance so it more closely matched his identity. My deep love for Lucas is the very same feeling I felt for Laura. But other facets of our relationship have been reimagined. I won't ever forget the day he invited me to help him shop for a men's suit! Having been raised as a girl, Luc is now experiencing the world through a young man's eyes, discovering male culture, with all its codes, biases, obligations, and privileges. In that sense, he understands me better than Laura ever could. Kathleen and I grieved the loss of Laura. But feelings of loss gave way to joy, because Lucas is a much happier person, more comfortable in his own skin, than Laura could ever hope to be.

Luc and I still enjoy hiking, fishing, and talking about sports. And, we are constantly reimagining, together, what it means to be in relationship – man to man. In that sense, he is the son I always had.

Dayna: Reimagining Mother's Day

I found my mom overdosed on prescription pain medication on Mother's Day 2006. It was her second relapse since the spring of 2002. That pivotal day marked for me an important milestone: I reimagined my life without my mom. It also led to reimagining a more mature, albeit complicated, relationship with my mom.

Everything slowed that Mother's Day, as it often does when a trauma is unfolding; I saw things with remarkable clarity. I finally understood that my mother's recovery from addiction was out of my control. I needed to get out of the way, so she could do the work – so she could choose sobriety for herself. I found the large plastic bag of prescription medication bottles behind her chair, gave it to the medics to take with them to the hospital, and in what felt like slow motion, I followed the ambulance out of my mom's neighborhood.

As the hospital staff prepared to pump my mom's stomach that day, I said to a nurse, "Let me know when you're going to start." "Squeamish, huh?" He poked at me a bit. "No, I've just decided, as of today, to spare myself a memory." As another nurse joined to help secure the restraints, I stepped to the bedside to help. The new nurse gently smiled and asked, "Is that your Mother's Day outfit?" I glanced down at my skirt with the flowered embroidery and nodded. "Do you have children?" she asked. "Yes, three." "How old are they?" "Thirteen, eleven, and six." She reached across my mom's stomach, grabbed ahold of my forearms, looked me directly in the eyes and said, "Take it from someone who knows. Go home to your kids. Let us take care of your mom." I replied, "I was only waiting for your signal that it was a good time for me to leave." Up until that day, I don't ever remember leaving a loved one at the hospital. I had always stuck it out until the bitter end.

Around that same time, I was introduced to my co-authors' forgiveness scholarship. My wise co-author Doug said to me, "Dayna, why does reconciliation need to be 'yes' or 'no'? Why can't it be one with boundaries?" Our conversation has guided so much of my thinking over the past 11 years.

Walking out of the hospital that day and creating some boundaries with my mom was pivotal to my own health and happiness. I am a more intentional mother to my kids because of that decision; I am a better partner to my husband, a more thoughtful friend, a more effective teacher and student, and a much better daughter. But perhaps most of all, I have so much more self-respect and inner peace because while I chose boundaries to our reconciliation, I also chose to stay connected to my mom. I realize this is not the same for everyone; many people embrace an all or nothing mindset toward relationships with loved ones who battle or have battled addiction. I'm so grateful I opted to reimagine.

Some quality, long overdue communication between my mom and me set the tone for our more mature mother–daughter relationship. When my mom first reached out to me after checking herself into rehab after her overdose, she shared what finally felt like the first real apology I'd ever received from her. She said she couldn't imagine how frightened I must have been to find her like that. I also tried a new communication strategy. I told her that historically my instinct had been to immediately respond, "It's okay", in order to ease her discomfort. But I added that I had recently learned more about communicating forgiveness and the careful difference between excusing, minimizing and forgiving. So this time, I thought I should instead acknowledge her apology and admit to her (and myself) just how painful and scary her close brush with death had been. I told her that I loved her and always would and said I'd like us to work toward forgiveness and reconciliation as I continued to understand more about what they both really meant. I also shared that I thought our mutual work should be done from a bit more distance than had become customary during my mom's crises.

The road to reimagining a healthier relationship with my mom has been a long journey over the past 11 years, one replete with many of my own missteps, recalibrations, abundant self-reflection, and third-party support. It has been complicated, as most people who love someone who battles addiction will also attest. But there has also been laughter, joy, warmth, and compassion that I would have missed had I severed all contact with her. On this past Christmas, our family roared laughing while playing a silly game; my kids (now ages 25, 23, and 17) saw a side of my mom they had never enjoyed before. My mom also cried when my brother opened a generous gift from my dad. And during a conversation a few weeks ago, my mom said to me, "I have three amazing grandkids. Dayna, you've done a great job raising three beautiful children."

What I most hope to convey to others through my narrative is how liberating it has been to have a more realistic and mature relationship with my mom. And in these middle years of my life, as I come to terms with my own abundant shortcomings as a mom, a wife, a teacher and student, a friend, and a daughter, I will continue to draw strength from my mom's courage, compassion, and resilience.

Doug: Reimagining a "Good" Marriage

My wife and I entered counseling in our 31st year of marriage, just six months after publication of my first, sole-authored book, *Marital Communication*. Life can be ironic. While I have never claimed to do marriage perfectly, the honest truth was that I thought our marriage was much better than most and that I really "got this stuff". After all, I have a Master of Counseling degree, my doctoral dissertation was focused on interpersonal and marital communication, and I have conducted countless relationship workshops on marriage and family issues. I had referred many people to counseling over my 20 years of teaching, but I never really felt like Ann and I needed it. When we occasionally broached the subject, I typically responded, "We can figure this out", "I actually think we're making good progress", "I like our marriage better than anyone else's I know. We'll be okay". So we never dealt with any of our festering issues, until a few years ago. We unexpectedly hit an impasse where deep hurt and dysfunctional patterns of behavior could no longer be ignored.

Our four years of intense counseling and relationship work (including a three-month separation while I was teaching *Family Communication* and our son was taking my course. Did I mention life can be ironic?) helped us reimagine the guiding narrative of our relationship. Three themes comprised a major portion of this narrative and had to be rethought and reconstructed: Nice is not necessarily loving, honoring is not necessarily respecting, forgiveness does not necessarily mean that people will change in the ways you want.

Ann and I are nice people – just ask us! My wife, as a last born, and I, as an only child, have often made our ways through life by being likeable and not rocking the boat with others. We are both positive human beings – stay nice, stay upbeat, and things will eventually work out. And we love each other, so we're nice to each other. Makes sense. Yet, our niceness almost killed our marriage. Essentially, our niceness often became a means of not being honest about how we felt and what we thought. In such times, our niceness was less about love than it was about avoiding the hard stuff. So there we were – our niceness, undetected, eroding the emotional connection in our marriage.

Respect is a huge issue in relationships. Got that. Not perfectly executed, but, nonetheless, high on the list of things Ann and I both knew we needed to offer one another. One day our counselor told us that without respect you will feel used in the relationship, especially when it comes to things that are based on a strong sense of mutuality . . . like sex. Okay, got that, too. Check. Then one day Ann told me that I had honored her in our marriage, but not respected her. Zing. Game changer. I had been doing all kinds of positive things (e.g., giving compliments), but many of our interactions were characterized by me trying to stay on top – often communicated through a subtle, or not so subtle, tone of voice. And, staying on top was my own way of grabbing at respect for who I am. In spite of all the positive things we were both doing in our marriage, the respect issue was slowly grinding down the sense of equity, balance, and full acceptance we needed to build a strong relationship as equal partners.

Finally, learning to respect one another – manifested as equality as partners – paved the way for forgiveness. Our respect problems had been complicating our ability to forgive, because neither of us felt fully accepted by the other. While we had to work through forgiving specific acts, even more we had to learn that forgiveness was not necessarily going to change us into the people we thought we wanted. This required letting go of a lot of expectations for each other and for our marriage. Somewhat counterintuitively, Ann and I both arrived at the conclusion that if our marriage was going to survive, we had to be willing to let it go. That is, forgiving each other "as is" could mean personal acceptance at the cost of no longer wanting the relationship. The relationship surety we lived with for years ("We'll never divorce") had allowed us to grow too independent from one another, no longer accepting (and embracing!) our differences in a grand adventure.

Over the past four years we have learned to reimagine these three relationship themes and, by consequence, ourselves. The reimagination process started with the choice to accept the other wholeheartedly and to forgive who we, individually and together, had become over the past 31 years. We were 21 (Ann) and 24 (Doug) years old on our wedding day, so we pretty much grew up together and made our mistakes together. Now it was time to reimagine our future – by reimagining ourselves – no longer locked into "comfortable" patterns of behavior that were undercutting our emotional connection. For me, a practical way this worked itself out was rejecting fatalistic thinking (e.g., "I am doomed to this for the rest of my life. Nothing will ever change"). Instead, I would remind myself of my commitment to work *with Ann*, embracing our differences, as each day we chose a healthier future.

Working toward a future we both wanted meant reimagining what *nice* really looks like. The nice we practiced before counseling was, in part, a conflict-avoidance technique. No more. Ann and I committed to being kind to each other (instead of nice), while being honest about our thoughts and feelings. Our new, honest kindness doesn't always feel good, but it draws us closer to each other, strengthens the emotional connection between us, and helps us to be optimistic about our future.

Finally, we choose to continue to honor one another ("You did a good job with the taxes", "What you said to our son was spot on"), while making sure that we are consistently communicating respect for the other through our words and actions. That has meant that as we accept and value each other – just as we are – we engage one another as equal partners. Interestingly, a primary way that has shown up is mindful listening – aware, focused, no judgment – as we honestly seek to value the other and her or his perspective. Today our marriage is not perfect, but it is strong and challenging and, often, exciting. Most importantly, our reimagined behavior with one another more truly reflects the love we feel.

★

The reimagination process for all three authors has been difficult, but definitely worth the effort. Most of the topics in this book have been experienced by at least one of us as we have committed to the recreation of ourselves, our partners, and our relationships. As such, we invite you to keep reading and to join us on an academic and personal journey of relationship discovery.

Note

1   Conversation after Wendy's incarceration for drugs, when Kayla was just 15 years old; adapted from the original transcript; White & Mullen, 2017).
2   We regularly reference this book using its subtitle, *Reimagining Our Relationships.*

References

Arendt, H. (1959). *The human condition.* Chicago, IL: The University of Chicago Press.

Canary, D. J., & Stafford, L. (1992). Relational maintenance strategies and equity in marriage. *Communication Monographs, 59,* 630–649.

Dempsey, S., Dutta, M., Frey, L. R., Goodall, H. L., Soyini Madison, D., Mercieca, J., . . . Miller, K. (2011). What is the role of the communication discipline in social justice, community engagement, and public scholarship? A visit to the CM Café. *Communication Monographs, 79,* 256–271.

Docan-Morgan, S. J. (2014) "They were strangers who loved me": Discussions, narratives, and rituals during Korean adoptees' initial reunions with birth families. *Journal of Family Communication, 14*(4), 352–373. doi:10.1080/15267431.2014.946033

Enright, R. D., Gassin, E. A., & Wu, C. R. (1992). Forgiveness: A developmental view. *Journal of Moral Education, 21,* 99–114.

Enright, R. D., & the Human Development Study Group. (1991). The moral development of forgiveness. In W. Kurtines & J. Gewirtz (Eds.), *Handbook of moral behavior and development* (pp. 123–152). Hillsdale, NJ: Lawrence Erlbaum.

Feeney, J. A. (2005). Hurt feelings in couple relationships: Exploring the role of attachment and perceptions of personal injury. *Personal Relationships, 12,* 253–271.

Feeney, J. A. (2009). When love hurts: Understanding hurtful events in couple relationships. In A. Vangelisti (Ed.), *Feeling hurt in close relationships* (pp. 313–335). New York, NY: Cambridge University Press.

Fehr, R., Gelfand, M. J., & Nag, M. (2010). The road to forgiveness: A meta-analytic synthesis of its situational and dispositional correlates. *Psychological Bulletin, 136,* 894–914.

Fincham, F. D. (2004). Communication in marriage. In A. L. Vangelisti (Ed.), *Handbook of family communication* (pp. 83–103). Mahwah, NJ: Lawrence Erlbaum.

Frey, L. R. (2009). Social justice. In S. W. Littlejohn & K. A. Foss (Eds.), *Encyclopedia of communication theory* (Vol. 2, pp. 908–911). Thousand Oaks, CA: Sage.

Frey, L. R., & Palmer, D. L. (2017). Communication activism pedagogy and research: Communication education scholarship to promote social justice. *Communication Education, 66,* 362–367.

Galvin, K. M. (2006). Diversity's impact on defining the family: Discourse dependence and identity. In R. West & L. H. Turner (Eds.), *The family communication sourcebook* (pp. 3–19). Thousand Oaks, CA: Sage.

Gordon, K. C., Baucom, D. H., & Snyder, D. K. (2004). An integrative intervention for promoting recovery from extramarital affairs. *Journal of Martial and Family Therapy, 30,* 213–231.

Gordon, K. C., Baucom, D. H., & Snyder, D. K. (2005). Treating couples recovering from infidelity: An integrative approach. *Journal of Clinical Psychology, 61,* 1393–1405.

Gottman, J. M. (1994). *What predicts divorce?* Hillsdale, NJ: Lawrence Erlbaum.

Guerrero, L., & Cole, M. (2015). Moral standards, emotions, and communication associated with relational transgressions in dating relationships. In V. Waldron & D. Kelley (Eds.),

Moral talk across the lifespan: Creating good relationships (pp. 155–182). New York, NY: Peter Lang.

Hargrave, T. D. (1994). Families and forgiveness: A theoretical and therapeutic framework. *The Family Journal: Counseling and Therapy for Couples and Families, 2*, 339–348.

Hargrave, T. D., & Sells, J. N. (1997). The development of a forgiveness scale. *Journal of Marital and Family Therapy, 23*, 41–63.

Hoad, T. (1986). Conciliate. In Hoad, T. F. (Ed.), *The concise Oxford dictionary of English etymology*. Oxford: Oxford University Press.

Honeycutt, J. M., & Wiemann, J. M. (1999). Analysis of functions of talk and reports of imagined interactions (IIs) during engagement and marriage. *Human Communication Research, 25*, 399–419.

Kelley, D. L. (1998). The communication of forgiveness. *Communication Studies, 49*, 255–271.

Kelley, D. L. (2012a). Forgiveness as restoration: The search for well-being, reconciliation, and relational justice. In T. J. Socha & M. J. Pitts (Eds.), *The positive side of interpersonal communication* (pp. 193–210). New York, NY: Peter Lang.

Kelley, D. L. (2012b). *Marital communication*. Cambridge, UK: Polity Press.

Kelley, D. L. (2012c). Prayer and forgiveness: Communication and Christian applications. *The Journal of Communication and Religion, 35*, 254–269.

Kelley, D. L. (2015). Chapter 4: Just relationships. In V. Waldron & D. Kelley (Eds.), *Moral talk across the lifespan: Creating good relationships* (pp. 75–94). New York, NY: Peter Lang.

Kelley, D. L. (2017). *Just relationships: Living out social justice as mentor, family, friend, and lover*. New York, NY: Routledge.

Kelley, D. L., & Burgoon, J. K. (1991). Understanding marital satisfaction and couple type as functions of relational expectations. *Human Communication Research, 18*, 40–69.

Kelley, D. L., & Waldron, V. R. (2005). An investigation of forgiveness-seeking communication and relational outcomes. *Communication Quarterly, 53*, 339–358.

Kloeber, D. N. (2011). Voicing conditional forgiveness. Arizona State University.

Kloeber, D. N., & Waldron, V. R. (2017). Expressing and suppressing conditional forgiveness in serious romantic relationships. In J. A. Samp (Ed.), *Communicating interpersonal conflict in close relationships: Contexts, challenges, and opportunities* (pp. 250–266). New York, NY: Routledge.

McCullough, M. E., Pargament, K. I., & Thoresen, C. E. (Eds.). (2000). *Forgiveness: Theory, research, and practice*. New York, NY: Guilford.

Merolla, A. J. (2008). Communicating forgiveness in friendships and dating relationships. *Communication Studies, 59*(2), 114-131.

Merolla, A. J. (2017). Forgiveness following conflict: What it is, why it happens, and how it's done. In J. A. Samp (Ed.), *Communicating interpersonal conflict in close relationships: Contexts, challenges, and opportunities* (pp. 227–249). New York, NY: Routledge.

Merolla, A. J., & Zhang, S. (2011). In the wake of transgression: Examining forgiveness communication in personal relationships. *Personal Relationships, 18*, 79–95. doi:10.1111/j.1475–6811.2010.01323.x

Metts, S. (1994). Relational transgressions. In W. R. Cupach & B. H. Spitzberg (Eds.), *The dark side of interpersonal communication* (pp. 217–239). Hillsdale, NJ: Lawrence Erlbaum.

Murphy, J. G., & Hampton, J. (1998). *Forgiveness and mercy*. Cambridge, UK: Cambridge University Press.

Putnam, L. L. (2006). Definitions and approaches to conflict and communication. In J. G. Oetzel & S. Ting-Toomey (Eds.), *The SAGE handbook of conflict communication: Integrating theory, research, and practice* (pp. 1–32). Thousand Oaks, CA: Sage.

Vangelisti, A. L. (2009). Hurt feelings: Distinguishing features, functions, and overview. In A. L. Vangelisti (Ed.), *Feeling hurt in close relationships* (pp. 3–11). New York, NY: Cambridge University Press.

Vangelisti, A. L., Young, S. L., Carpenter-Theune, K. E., & Alexander, A. L. (2005). Why does it hurt? The perceived causes of hurt feelings. *Communication Research, 32,* 443–477.

Waldron, V. R., & Kelley, D. L. (2005). Forgiveness as a response to relational transgression. *Journal of Social and Personal Relationships, 22,* 723–742.

Waldron, V. R., & Kelley, D. L. (2008). *Communicating forgiveness.* Thousand Oaks, CA: Sage.

Waldron, V. R., & Kelley, D. L. (2015). *Moral talk across the lifespan: Creating good relationships.* New York, NY: Peter Lang.

White, J., & Mullen, M. (2017, January). *Do you remember the day you were released from prison and got to come home?* Available from storycorps.org

Worthington, E. L., Jr. (1998). An empathy-humility-commitment model of forgiveness applied within family dyads. *Journal of Family Therapy, 20,* 59–76.

Worthington, E. L., Jr. (2001). Unforgiveness, forgiveness, and reconciliation and their implications for societal interventions. In R. G. Helmick & R. L. Petersen (Eds.), *Forgiveness and reconciliation* (pp. 171–192). Philadelphia. PA: Templeton Foundation Press.

Yoshimura, S. M., & Boon, S. D. (2018). *Communicating revenge in interpersonal relationships.* London, UK: Lexington Books.

2

CULTIVATING RELATIONAL CREATIVITY

Raj was in his early 30s, having spent the years since college traveling the country for the rapidly growing technology company that hired him into their marketing department. The company embraced a "work hard, play hard" culture, and Raj spent most of his off hours with coworkers, enjoying local breweries, and competing in company-sponsored sports leagues. In fact, he met Jessica at a softball game and he quickly became enamored with her fun-loving spirit, sharp wit, and competitive drive. Jess was a software engineer, charged with bug-testing new products before they were released to consumers. She loved the work, but her job was demanding, requiring 60 hours a week when a product release was upcoming. After the season ended, the pair stayed in touch, started dating in their precious spare moments, and eventually became quite serious. Over the course of a year, Raj and Jessica became a "thing" around the company and they started talking about how a shared future might look for such a busy couple. Jess confessed that she hoped to have kids someday, much to Raj's relief, as he too dreamed of being a parent. But Jess knew she would always maintain her career and worried that she might not have time to be a parent unless her partner accepted much of the caregiving responsibility. Raj wondered if he could be that person. Tired of hurried dates and abbreviated weekends, he was certainly ready to give up the travel to accept a slower-paced job. Then the couple might be able to date like "normal people" and really get to know each other. If that worked out, could he set his career aside to be a full-time parent? Raj wasn't completely sure, but he wanted his relationship with Jess to grow much deeper, and their conversations about the future were stirring his imagination.

★

Reimagining Our Relationships is based on the premise that it is healthy for us to reassess what has felt "natural" in our relationships, especially when things go "wrong". In the case of Raj and Jess, what seems wrong is a growing uncertainty between career and relational goals. The somewhat frenetic relationship pace they kept during the early stages of the relationship seems unsustainable as they consider long-term commitment to one another and even children. To have the future they want, Jess and Raj are reimagining their relationship, but wondering if they have the ability to make this really work.

The lucky among us have trusted friends or mentors with whom it is safe to explore our relational histories, hopes, and hesitations. But, as was the case with this busy pair, most of us "fall into" relationships, relating intuitively as friends and lovers. Relational expectations may not be all that clear, even to ourselves. Instead, we enact patterns modeled by our parents or simply absorbed from the cultural milieu in which we were raised. Through these processes of relational socialization, we learn explicit relationship rules (e.g., "Look at me when I talk to you"), notice implicit relationship norms (e.g., "No public displays of affection"), and sometimes grow accustomed to unhealthy patterns of behavior, such as verbal or physical aggression or "the silent treatment". Our partners do too.

Yet, as the opening scenario demonstrates, at various points in our adult lives it becomes necessary for each of us to examine critically our assumptions about relationships – intentionally building on the positive elements of what we have learned up until now, and reinventing those aspects that are unsatisfying, unhealthy, or simply no longer "working" as we grow in age, experience, and insight.

Relationship development is an art, a collaborative process of creation in which partners transform the raw materials of relationships into something unique and even inspired. In this chapter, we explore this creative process as we identify metaphors useful to the reconceptualization of our personal connections, describe rich sources of relational imagination capable of being mined for fresh ideas and perspectives, offer concrete suggestions that guide the reimagination process, and offer a definition of relationship reimagination that frames this entire inspired enterprise. We begin with the latter.

A Definition of Relationship Reimagination

Two decades of engaging people, hurting and confused in their relationships, struggling to move forward, has resulted in the identification of a process we are calling *relationship reimagination*. This approach to understanding relationship change emphasizes the role of language and meaning (metaphor), models and sources of imagination (sources of change), and the qualities of interpersonal interactions that help evaluate past behaviors and define a hopeful future. To this end, we offer the following definition, followed by a discussion of possible means for drawing on your imagination in the midst of relationship turmoil.

> *Relationship reimagination is a process whereby existing and past patterns of relational behavior are recognized by one or both partners; metaphors and sources*

of change are explored and the current emotional, behavioral, and moral meanings of the relationship are reevaluated. Through dialogue, partners experience shifts in perspective and emotion, leading to the reimagination of their individual selves and their possible joint relational future. With hope, time, and practice, they forge a new reality characterized by benevolent and just communication.

The first means of integrating reimagination into your relationships is perhaps the most obvious – talk with your family members, romantic partners, or friends about the patterns of behavior that have characterized your relationship up until now. Putting your past into words with your relational partner can be an imaginative, negotiated process – memory is as much recreation as it is recall. Because it is often difficult to put our relational experiences into words, talking and thinking with metaphors can be a means of creating mutual understanding. One of Doug's counseling professors (Dr. Johnson) recounted the following story about Jan and Darnell, who had come to a weekend workshop for distressed couples. Dr. Johnson began the workshop with a trust-building experience – one partner is blindfolded and the other partner leads them around the facility as they talk about their week. They then trade places. Jan and Darnell had a little trouble getting the blindfold around Jan's hair and so were the last to leave the room. As Darnell guided Jan through the double doors, he pushed the door on his side open and absently-mindedly ran his wife square into the other door. She threw off the blindfold and screamed at him, "That's what you've been doing to me our entire marriage!" As unfortunate as this story is, it was a turning point for Darnell. They had tried to rationally talk through their problems for years, but until this living metaphor occurred, he never really understood her experience.

Describing the behavior, thoughts, and feelings that stand out as you recall your past can also help your partner imagine and empathize with your experience. This metaphorical backward look might reveal behavioral patterns that left you feeling dissatisfied. Perhaps you felt "locked into" certain routines, "trapped" by the roles you were expected to play, or "forced" into practices that made you feel uncomfortable. Emotions are often what make our past memorable, so try to put those emotions into words. Did you feel disappointed, fearful, frustrated, guilty, dissatisfied, disrespected? What thoughts were you experiencing then? Were you wishing for something different? Imagining conversations you wanted to have, but could not? Experiencing doubts about yourself or those around you? In Vince's case, his past relationship with Lucas often seemed like a puzzle or a mystery. Lucas wasn't always sure how to describe his evolving gender and sexual identity, and Vince lacked some important pieces of information that might have helped. For example, Vince had close contacts with friends who identified as gay, but transgender people remained a mystery. Unlike a game, however, this puzzle was freighted with emotion, including Luc's fear of rejection by friends and family and Vince's feeling of inadequacy in the face of his son's anxiety and depression.

Understanding the past as an unsolved puzzle is helpful to Vince and Lucas because they see that both parties were trying valiantly to make sense of a picture that remained incomplete, not because of their own failures, but because their personal experiences had yielded few hints about the solution that would emerge as Lucas sorted through the clues to his identity.

Second, the reimagination process can be used to characterize how you view the relationship now, and how you want it to look in the future. In recent times, Vince has learned to take his cues from Lucas. For example, Luc explained how important it was for his family to use the correct pronoun ("he") and his chosen name, even when talking about the past. And Luc has asked questions about living responsibly as a "male" in a world that often privileges masculinity and hyper-sexualizes women, a task that is challenging for Vince as well. A future of sharing questions and working to solve puzzles is one that appeals to both of them because it describes a relationship that feels more open, less strained, and more fun than what they experienced in the past.

Third, you may find that metaphors spark new dialogue about the future. If the past has disappointed you, a *metaphor of redemption* may direct your con-versations to the values and commitments that will make you feel good about your relationship again. Use your moral imagination to see the world as your partner might, thinking about how his or her gender socialization, family upbringing, career plans, and religious influences are both different from, and similar to, yours. If you recognize that your relational past was limited by a lack of knowledge or communication skills, a *metaphor of growth* might encourage you to seek counseling or education that will cultivate relational strengths. If you have survived hard times, a *forging* metaphor may prove useful as you consider how the difficulties of the past have molded and steeled you for challenges that loom ahead. Your willingness to have these metaphor-guided relational dialogues may in itself provide resilience to your relationships, because metacommunicative practices of this type can have protective and coping effects when partners encounter adversity in the future (Beck, 2016).

At this point, you might be thinking "I'm just not an imaginative person" or "This sounds interesting, but I'm unsure how to start" or, even, "I'm still unsure if imagination is that important to healing my damaged relationship". To help, we offer a few metaphors as ways to begin the reimagination process and, then, finish our discussion by examining potential sources of imagination from our daily lives.

Metaphors and Relational Imagination

The language we use to describe our relationships shapes our capacity to think about them differently (Lakoff & Johnson, 1980/2003). Scholars of organizational life have long noticed that workers can feel both constrained and empowered by the metaphors used by employers to describe workplace relations, such as references to "the team" or "our family" (Pondy, 1983; Turnage, 2013). If we listen carefully, we notice that metaphors are often invoked to describe our personal relationships, including the conflicts that inevitably occur in most friendships, families, and romantic couples. Dayna's story evokes vivid metaphors to describe her reimagined relationship with her mom. These images describe new ways of interacting with one another (long journey, boundary setting, liberating), and reveal a new understanding of their complex relationship. In their oft-used textbook, conflict scholars Joyce Hocker and Bill Wilmot (2017) identify numerous metaphors for interpersonal conflict. For some, conflict is associated with deeply negative meanings. They are "at war" with their partners or family members, locked in battle while awaiting the next explosive interchange, apprehensive at the prospective of volcanic emotions and explosive disagreements. The meanings conjured by these phrases are often rooted in a family history of destructive conflict, a past that shapes current behavior, sometimes without full awareness. Of course, more constructive conflict metaphors are also used by couples and families. For some, conflict is a matter of "working things out", "solving the puzzle", or "getting back in sync". This language frames conflict as a challenge, but one that is welcomed because it leads to increased understanding and smoother relational functioning.

Beyond the role of framing conflicts, relational metaphors are often invoked to tell the story of a relationship, to interpret its path from past to present and on into the future (Glucksberg & McGlone, 1999). Communication scholar Patrice Buzzenell has proposed a communicative theory of resilience that emphasizes the role of discourse in reshaping and stabilizing relationships after periods of disruption or change. In one interesting study of families experiencing economic hard times, it was observed that parents stabilized their families by invoking metaphors that emphasized their strength and adaptability (Lucas & Buzzanell, 2012). In resilient families, children learn that the family unit will persevere by "tightening the belt" or that it will "bend but not break". These and other metaphors help kids experience stability during times of change even as they convey that family life must be adapted.

Beck (2016) proposes a model of relational resilience that emphasizes both proactive (e.g., dreaming together about the future, planning ahead) and reactive (forgiving past mistakes, conserving resources) strategies that help partners adapt constructively to stressors and disruptive events. Recently, Waldron (2017) identified metaphoric examples of such practices that surfaced in interviews with nearly 300 midlife romantic couples who had been together for more than 20 years. His research team wondered how these veteran partnerships had weathered significant midlife challenges, such as the onset of serious illness, the "empty nest" (notice the metaphor), difficulties with adult offspring, and job loss. Using the technique of root metaphor analysis (for an early example, see Smith & Eisenberg, 1987), the researchers identified several foundational meanings that pervaded the stories couples told about their relationships. Some of these suggested that, at midlife, the partnerships were protected by investments made in the past. These couples described themselves as fully invested, grounded in a time-tested trust, prepared by past encounters with adversity. They had forged "unbreakable bonds". Other couples invoked metaphors of coping and adjustment. During a challenging period of life they were battling the forces that threatened to pull them apart, trying to run a marathon (not a sprint), and fine tuning their roles and practices. When bad news surfaced, these couples preferred "dealing with" unpleasant realities rather than avoiding or delaying. In contrast, another collection of couples described their relationship with metaphors that suggested they were thriving in the face of midlife adversity. They invoked images of growth, adventure, and, in the wake of serious transgressions, redemption.

As Waldron's study revealed, metaphors need not just reference the relational past and present. Instead they can be invoked strategically to help us imagine how our relationships might change, preparing us for a different future. We certainly see this in clinical settings, when therapists help clients replace constricting language with metaphors that open up new possibilities. For example, Mount and Moas (2015) argued that the metaphor of "the empty nest" created an unnecessarily bleak and restrictive view of the post-parenting years. They describe a therapeutic technique that encourages couples to describe "chapters" in the story of their lives and to "repurpose" the empty nest idea. For some, the post-parenting chapter might be reimagined as a period of self-nurturing or an opportunity to develop talents that had been neglected when the nest was crowded with chicks.

The experience of unexpected change can make familiar metaphors feel inadequate and deprive them of their meaning. In our previous work, partners who experienced infidelity described being "crushed" as the foundations of their most solid relationships (trust, loyalty) crumbled around them (Waldron & Kelley, 2008). At home, and at work, the sometimes disconcerting experience of change can feel like a "rug has been pulled out" from under one's feet. Of course, the meaning of change can be filtered through a more optimistic metaphorical lens. It can release us from the grip of an overly needy partner, help us breathe after a stultifying period of relational staleness, or prompt us to take inventory of our "true" friends while discarding bonds that have proven to be burdensome or unhealthy. And despite searing pain, a breakup sometimes forges a stronger, more resilient person, one who is better able to withstand the vicissitudes of relational life.

So change is not always welcome in personal relationships, but often we discover it to be a long-awaited friend. In order to better welcome the relationship transitions that characterize all human relationships, we think it is helpful to broaden the vocabulary of change, exploring metaphors that can both describe and guide relational transformation. Indeed, language is a primary resource in the definition of relationship imagination suggested in this chapter. Here are some of the metaphors we find helpful (later, in *Chapter 8*, we discuss the metaphor of "forgiveness tree" in depth).

Reimagining. Often associated with the work of artists, architects, and science fiction writers, reimagination is the root metaphor that informs this text. To use our imagination is to conjure new possibilities for our relationship, to craft an unsoiled version of the relational future. Reimagining involves a willingness to let go of assumed, taken for granted roles, norms, and, expectations. It calls us to let go of the familiar: To dream, concoct, invent. A reimagined marriage might look quite different as couples learn to share roles that were previously owned by a single partner, roles such as bread winner, caregiver, or sexual initiator. A reimagined parent–child relationship might be one in which adult offspring share roles once owned by parents: Providing advice, initiating communication, looking after their well-being, helping them stay afloat during a financial crisis. A reimagined sibling relationship could involve the recasting of traditional expectations based on birth order, with new arrangements based on siblings' common interests and talents or their desire to play leading or supporting roles in the larger family. Of course, these kinds of reimaginings require recognition that existing arrangements, though familiar, are no longer satisfying and certainly not optimal. And it may require courage, trust, and a mutual commitment to maintain valued bonds even as they are radically transformed.

Forging. We invoke this term as it is used by metalworkers. A forge is a furnace, a hearth in which metals are melted, impurities separated, and materials shaped into new forms. Relationships, at times, involve the melding of needs, wants, and styles, and, when things go well, assuming new and stronger forms after periods of heated conflict and scorched feelings. Couples sometimes forge more honest, satisfying, and intimate connections after they have been "burned" by such adversities as financial irresponsibility, unsustainable habits of overwork, or even infidelity. Families may forge stronger relationships as they collectively cope with the serious illness of a parent or rally to the side of a sibling who is experiencing unwelcome divorce. The strengths of individual members are melded in such cases, and petty disagreements of the past may melt into insignificance. These partnerships may be forever strengthened as the story of this process is retold and embellished.

Of course, as any blacksmith knows, fire is a fickle and mercurial partner in the forging process. It can cause painful burns and yield lasting imperfections in the finished product. In this way, painful past experiences can leave indelible burns in our relational memory. These include deeply held grudges about perceived betrayals, unsupportive family members, friends who failed us in moments of need. The forging metaphor reminds us that to create relationships of integrity we may need to first locate and melt away the resentments that are best relegated to the past.

Renewing. The metaphor of renewal invites us to reclaim and revitalize what has been good in our relationships. It calls us to examine critically the current state of our connections with others, to wonder what has been lost or changed with the passing of time and the accumulation of experience. Renewal can imply a fresh start, a mindful "reset", a willingness to reinvest in your friendship, romantic partnership, coworker relationship, or family. Of course, it takes effort to do so and it may require you to let "bygones be bygones". Renewal is sometimes a formal process, as when veteran couples choose to renew their marriage vows in a public ceremony. But renewal is more often informal and private. Friends who have drifted apart decide to restart their relationship by connecting on Facebook and then meeting for coffee. Lovers rekindle their passion by putting work aside and scheduling a weekend alone. Extended families decide it has been too long since "we were all together" and begin planning for a family reunion. In each case, it has become obvious that something valued has been neglected, that the emotional wellspring that is our relationships must be collectively tended to, recharged, replenished, and reclaimed. These activities assure that what has been valued in the past will be sustained into the future.

Redeeming. This metaphor is deeply rooted in the idea that things can be restored to their original purpose. Doug keeps a soda bottle in his office that is printed on the back: *Redemption Value 5 cents* – a used, empty bottle to be restored to its original purpose. So too our closest relationships are sites of redemption and transformation. Feeling emotionally "used up" and empty, partners and relationships explore new ways to heal and be full once again.

McAdams (2006) has explored the nature of redemptive narratives, finding that people who find meaning in past mistakes may be more resilient, willing to invest in new relationships. Indeed, redemptive conversations help us reshape the future even as we recover from the past. We redeem ourselves when we make things right, live up to our promise, reaffirm our commitment to personal and relational values, show that we have learned and grown from the experience of letting others down. Redemption is a process of rediscovering our own goodness and helping others believe in us once again. It is often said that we are most likely to hurt the people we love. But the flipside of that idea is this – those we love best know our potential. It is our friends, after all, who know us well and like us despite our faults. It is our romantic partners who have invested deeply in us and are often willing to be patient until that investment proves worthwhile. It is often our family members who are rooting for us to do better and often willing to be patient just because "we are family".

Redemption is a process of emotional repair and relational rethinking. It is a future-oriented process that requires us to place mistakes in the past and commit to a new beginning. It is hopeful in the sense that it replaces simplistic ideas of relationship perfection with a more complex viewpoint that recognizes perfection in imperfection. We are who we are *because of the mistakes we've made and how we have reimagined who we are*, not because we have never made mistakes. For those who have disappointed, it requires humility, self-reflection, and resolve. For those who have been disappointed, it requires patience and benevolence.

In relationships, the possibility of redemption brings hope that a damaged relationship will be restored, that damaged partners will be restored.

Healing. The metaphor of healing is drawn from medicine where physicians strive to mend broken bones and restore the patient to good health. Broken bones hurt and, sometimes, relationships do too. The healing metaphor has been widely explored (for an intriguing discussion of its advantages and limitations, see Paré, Young, Freedman, Scott, & Behan, 2006). This way of thinking about relationships draws our attention to the roles played by patience, self-care, and therapy. Emotional wounds take time to heal and they can become inflamed if we ignore them or fail to seek the therapy of supportive friends and trusted confidants. However, the human body and psyche are designed for healing. When we get our bodies and minds into right alignment, healing becomes a natural process (Doidge, 2015; Weil, 1995). For instance, when your authors were younger, Western medicine's common approach to mending a broken arm was to put it in a cast. Today, doctors are much more likely to use less intrusive support and let the arm's own weight naturally align the break for healing. On the other hand, with severe breaks, more intrusive measures by a third party may be necessary to set the damaged area.

When we hurt others, healing may be facilitated by recognizing the damage we have done, offering sincere apologies, pledging improvement, and allowing them time to recover. Alternatively, we may use a third party to help us reset the relationship so that healing can begin to naturally occur. When healed properly, broken bones and relationships can be good as new. Restored to health we may feel more committed to living well, to avoiding situations that unwisely compromise our well-being. Similarly, emotional healing may leave us feeling more attuned to the health of our relationships – better able to recognize the behaviors that hurt ourselves and others, more aware of the vulnerability of even our strongest relationships.

Growing. Borrowed from the developmental processes of nature, the metaphor of growth emphasizes adaptation, learning, deepening our roots. One of us consulted an arborist when, a year after planting, a tree appeared sickly. After a few moments of inspection, the specialist noted that the sapling was still tethered to wooden supports intended to protect it from the gusting winds of the desert storms that visited our area in late summer. Untie the tree, she advised, and let it draw strength from its own roots. Only then would the roots respond by extending their reach more deeply into the soil. Sure enough, in coming months the once-shaky tree became more steady, its branches reached skyward, thriving on sunlight, and the trunk thickened.

If young relationships can be imagined from this perspective, they might be encouraged to grow outward, drawing sustenance from the outside as well as the supports provided by the partners themselves. It would be recognized that exposure to some degree of adversity is natural, that challenging winds can encourage us to dig our roots more deeply in the soils of love and trust, that the base of our relationship is expanded when we release ourselves from restrictive expectations and come to know our partners more deeply and realistically.

This metaphor of growth melds nicely with notions of learning. As when we were children learning to spell, our early clumsy efforts are essential to our development. If we had failed to learn from our mistakes, we would be spelling poorly later in life. Mistakes are not harbingers of permanent failure. Nor are they moral deficiencies. Rather they are opportunities to grow, mature, and learn. Guided by the metaphor of growth, we might approach future relationships with a learning attitude, one that values the lessons of the past while also recognizing that new (and renewed) relationships call us to change and mature.

A Caution on the Use of Metaphor

Metaphors highlight certain features of relationships and tend to push others into the background. In using them, we should be aware of both qualities. And as helpful as they can be, metaphors should be fully explored and even contested in our conversations. For example, the metaphor of healing implies that someone or some relationship is broken, hurting, or sick. Is that really the case? It could be that healing is needed even among people who are relatively healthy, because even in highly functioning families or relationships it is not uncommon for people to be hurt, even if that hurt is unintentional. The metaphor of redemption is quite hopeful, but it should not obscure the importance of past mistakes, the possibility that they may occur again, and the need for genuine acknowledgment of wrongdoing when that has occurred (Waldron & Kelley, 2008). All of this is to say that metaphors should be discussed and explored, not imposed or accepted uncritically. Indeed, it makes good sense to listen to metaphors that occur "naturally" as you discuss relationships, and then compare and contrast a variety of alternative ways of thinking.

Sources of Relational Imagination

Reimagining relationships can be challenging; thankfully, however, the uses of imagination are familiar to most of us. For example, it is not uncommon to imagine what a future career might involve. And most of us are familiar with the act of daydreaming. If you belong to a religious community, you might have been encouraged to imagine what a better world might look like, in the present or in the hereafter. In sports, such as baseball, it is not uncommon for fans of failing teams to imagine a better future, one that is simply delayed until "next season". Recently, the Chicago Cubs actually won the World Series after decades of futile effort. Through imagination, Cubs fans remained hopeful that their hapless team would eventually find its way. So when we struggle to be imaginative in our relationships, it might help to look around us to find good models of imaginative thinking. Below we address just a few possibilities.

The Arts: Lessons From the Theater

Art can offer a realistic depiction of life, as we find in the tradition of realism. Representational art finds its power in its capacity to stir powerful feelings of recognition and identification. And yet, art also functions to help us transcend present moments, adopt new frames of reference, or just as important, view familiar circumstances from different perspectives. We often need help imagining our present relational realities, including the problems that we have tended to gloss over as well as the positive qualities that we take for granted. And yet at times we need to try out new ways of viewing relationships. Perhaps, as in an impressionist painting, we need to use imagination to soften the edges of our expectations about gender roles, sexual intimacy, or the "kind of person" we will admit into our circle of friends.

We tend to think of artists as wildly creative, as unstructured and unbound in their approach. But as a study of highly original theater directors reveals, creativity may actually flow from efforts to be imaginative *within* boundaries (Ibbotson & Darso, 2008). After systematically interviewing and observing directors, the researchers reported that these professionals create art within an environment of constraints: Tight budgets, scripts, demanding timelines, the complex requirements of stage and costume designers, the skillsets of actors, and the expectations of potential audiences. Indeed, successful directors proceed by first acknowledging "creative constraints". Imagination comes into play as director and actors find ways to create powerful and innovative performances while questioning, stretching, pushing, and renegotiating but never violating these boundaries. Constraints are not cookie-cutter molds within which actors must perform. Rather, they are challenges to the actor's talents, interpretations, and imagination. As one of us has written elsewhere, "actors might be told that a character must convey a convincing sense of emotional desperation or that a scene should make the audience quake in their boots. But the actors are not told how to make the emotion convincing or the audience afraid. Good actors are motivated by these challenges, and they frequently create performances that are so unique that even the director could not have imagined them" (Waldron & Kassing, 2017, p. 230).

Improvisational theater is another venue that showcases how imagination can be fostered within the boundaries that we set for ourselves and those that are imposed on us by the other actors on stage, as well as the audience response. Doug's experiences with improvisation put him in deep touch with inhibitions he placed on himself, but also forced him to learn how to respond creatively to the other actors on stage. Interestingly, over time the players develop somewhat predictable patterns interwoven with wonderful moments of novelty and creativity. As we discuss in *Chapter 5: Sense-making: Understanding Relational Change*, our personal relationships are wonderfully characterized by the balance between predictability and novelty. Predictability and novelty may be seen in the creative co-creation of relational principles that serve to stabilize the relationship. For some couples, those include honest expression of emotions, equality in the performance of relational tasks, or the rejection of corporal punishment in parenting. For others, sexual fidelity or support for the partners' careers may be fundamental. Having agreed to these boundary conditions, couples are free to imagine a relationship that works.

Faith as a Source of Reimagined Relationships

Although religious experience takes many forms, it typically involves faith of some kind. Faith is a word that implies trust in something. Many religious people experience a faith in God, and with that faith comes trust that God will provide, and that in the long run, faith will be rewarded with a better life in the hereafter. Praying is an expression of that faith and for some an exercise in imagining a better future. When people pray they may ask for guidance in uncertain times, for perseverance in the face of difficulty, or for forgiveness on the path to a better life. In a sense, these acts pray a desired future "into being", as penitents imagine what the future holds and ready themselves by creating something different spiritually within or in the material world.

For others, such as Buddhists, spiritual reflection reimagines the present. What would it be like if we could be radically accepting of the present, fully mindful, intensely present for those with whom we interact? Here, faith is a trust that enlightenment and peace follow from reflection and acceptance. Vince is a member of a Unitarian Universalist congregation. From within this spiritual tradition, reimagination comes not from envisioning a world in which a particular God rules, but one in which people live in respectful relationships, united by shared commitments to the dignity of the individual, love for all, and an open-ended search for meaning and truth. Here faith is invested in humanitarian values and the principles which foster peaceful and meaningful relationships.

Within many faith perspectives imagination emerges through prayer and empathy (Eidenmuller & Honeycutt, 2010) and the ability "to see one's self as not wholly injured or the perpetrator as wholly bad or evil, resulting in one's self and one's perpetrator becoming 'human' again" (Kelley, 2012, p. 262). This process of rehumanizing both self and other may create a deep sense of hope with the perceived possibility of relationship change. Embedded in forces (God; enlightenment; a caring community of others) that are larger than our own efforts, we are free to imagine a future that is larger than our own selves.

Empathy and the Moral Imagination

Philosophers have long grappled with the reality that people often behave in ways that are selfish and sometimes even hurtful to others. Is it possible to imagine a world in which this self-interested approach is displaced by one that balances our interest with those of others and the larger common good? Philosopher Martin Buber is notable for imagining such a world, one that would be achieved only when people engage in true *dialogue*. To have a dialogue, a meaningful conversation grounded in efforts to achieve shared understanding, requires us to imagine the lived experience of those we engage with, a process he called "imagining the real".

> . . . imagining the real means that I imagine to myself what another man [person] is at this very moment wishing, feeling, perceiving, thinking, and not as a detached content but in his [or her] very reality, that is, as a living process . . .
>
> (Buber, 1951, p. 112)

You may recognize that Buber's process is similar to what social scientists now describe as empathy. Malcolm, Warwar, and Greenberg (2005) propose that "affective empathy" can be understood as using one's imagination to understand what another person may be, or have been, feeling when they took an action that affected you for better or for worse.

It is sometimes difficult to be empathetic because we perceive others to be so different from us. Their actions are sometimes indecipherable and sometimes they just seem so *wrong*. And yet, it is by imagining the lived experience of others that we come to understand the moral standards that guide our own behavior. This is the *moral imagination*. Without it, we construe the world as if only our own experiences have been worthwhile, and the principles that guide us in our relationships remain protected from scrutiny. Imagining that others may live worthy lives helps us remain tolerant. And tolerance allows us to consider a broader range of possibilities, to engage in dialogue before we render judgment.

Andrew Fiala (2003) explores the intersections of imagination and tolerance on one hand and the need to make moral distinctions on the other. We tolerate others, including friends and partners who displease us, in part because we can imagine how their situation in the world – their life experiences, truths, and values – led them to view things differently. To the extent that we can see this, we will be more careful in our judgments of them, and perhaps open to changing our own views or finding some creative synthesis of these differing perspectives. Tolerance is the withholding or tempering of judgment as we probe for a deeper knowing of others and their situations.

As Fiala notes, it is often not possible to fully imagine the experience of others. He gives the example of sati, the Hindu practice by which widows cast themselves upon the funeral pyre of their departed husbands. Perhaps we can imagine the grief of a widow or her sense that life is not worth living without her husband, or her belief that she will be reunited with him after death. But Fiala finds it difficult to imagine that a widow would *voluntarily* choose to burn herself to death. It is possible for him to imagine that she devalues her life due to her immersion in a religious framework organized by men, one that convinces her to devalue her own life even as it encourages women to great sacrifice. In a sense this is a "failure" of the moral imagination that makes it difficult to tolerate the practice of sati. But the example also illustrates that even if we are able to imagine the widow's perspective, we must ultimately make judgments based on our own understandings of right and good ways to respond to a partner's death.

This presumes that we are aware of our own moral understandings. Have we really reflected on the moral commitments we want from ourselves and our partners? This self-knowledge also requires imagination because it forces us to consider situations that might challenge or change these commitments. Sometimes this is nearly impossible because life itself is unpredictable. I may have strong feelings about the proper response to sexual infidelity, but how will I respond if it happens well into the future, when I have invested years or decades in a marriage? What if I am the one who succumbs to temptation? Childless, I may be convinced that "honesty is the best policy" but will I be honest with my child when describing the indiscretions of my own youth? These practices in imagin-ation help us solidify our values, probe their boundaries, and anticipate the real-life complexities that we will face in our relationships. We will also likely discover that some of these questions will be fully answerable only later, by a version of us that has lived longer, known more people well, and experienced life more fully. Interestingly, this kind of reflection may help us in the task of imagining the truths and values of others. Imagining how experience will shape our moral commitments is not so different from imagining how the experiences of others shaped theirs.

The call of the moral imagination encourages us to deepen our understanding of burning brides and other mysterious (to us) practices and viewpoints. In doing so, we may come to see people and their situations differently; we may even come to appreciate and respect them or, alternatively, criticize them on firmer intellectual or moral grounds. We have more common ground with most of our relational mysteries. Understanding may emerge in frank and respectful conversations. Why does my partner seem cautious or anxious about sex? Perhaps she is among the many women who have experienced sexual exploitation by men or been shamed as a "slut" for pursuing sexual pleasure. Why does my partner view the disciplining of children so differently than I? Vince and spouse Kathleen shared a belief that corporal punishment of their daughters should be avoided because it transmitted to children the idea that adults deal with conflict through physical rather than verbal means. But, in desperation, Vince once resorted to spanking an unruly male nephew who was visiting the house. It was only upon later discussion that the couple realized that Vince was replicating a pattern he had experienced as a boy growing up in a house of male siblings and a father who believed that boys occasionally required physical punishment.

Final Imaginative Thoughts

We have made our case for the need to cultivate imagination as part of engaging positive relationship change. We finish this section by grounding what may too easily become an imagination "magic carpet" ride. A focus on imagination runs the risk of becoming lost in fantasy that serves to escape actualities, rather than engage our challenging relationship realities. Reimagination is more than a cognitive exercise. To alter relationships, we must alter our *practices*, seeking ways to make our relationships more just, benevolent, and satisfying. For some of us, this means learning to really listen before speaking. For others, it means admitting mistakes more freely and acknowledging such admissions more graciously. For others, still, the keys are found in such practices as putting emotions to words, offering positive recognition, curbing the tendency to give advice, remaining constructive during conflict, or being more welcoming to new ideas. These new practices take time, patience, and commitment, but relationships are unlikely to change if our behaviors remain the same. *Part II: Imaginative Work: Preparing for Change* takes us squarely into the process of imagining change by focusing on our responses to relationship disruption, experience and management of emotions, and attempts to make sense of a newly disrupted world.

References

Beck, G. A. (2016). Surviving involuntary unemployment together: The role of resilience-promoting communication in familial and committed relationships. *Journal of Family Communication, 16*(4), 369–385.

Buber, M. (1951). Distance and relation. *Hibbert Journal, 49*(2), 105–113.

Doidge, N. (2015). *The brain's way of healing: Remarkable discoveries and recoveries from the frontiers of neuroplasticity.* New York, NY: Penguin Books.

Eidenmuller, M. E., & Honeycutt, J. M. (2010). Characteristics and functions of imagined interactions compared to interpersonal prayer. In J. M. Honeycutt (Ed.), *Imagine that: Studies in imagined interaction.* New York, NY: Hampton Press.

Fiala, A. (2003). Toleration and the limits of the moral imagination. *Philosophy in the Contemporary World, 10*(2), 33–40. doi:10.5840/pcw200310216

Glucksberg, S., & McGlone, M. S. (1999). When love is not a journey: What metaphors mean. *Journal of Pragmatics, 31*(12), 1541–1558. doi:10.1016/S0378–2166(99)00003-X

Hocker, J. L., & Wilmot, W. W. (2017). *Interpersonal conflict.* New York, NY: McGraw-Hill Education.

Ibbotson, P., & Darso, L. (2008). Directing creativity: The art and craft of creative leadership. *Journal of Management & Organization, 14*(5), 548–559. doi:10.1017/S1833367200003035

Kelley, D. L. (2012). Prayer and forgiveness: Communication and Christian applications. *Journal of Communication and Religion, 35*, 254–269.

Lakoff, G., & Johnson, M. (Ed.). (2003). *Metaphors we live by*. Chicago, IL: The University of Chicago Press. (Original work published 1980)

Lucas, K., & Buzzanell, P. M. (2012). Memorable messages of hard times: Constructing short- and long-term resiliences through family communication. *Journal of Family Communication, 12*, 189–208. doi:10.1080/15267431.2012.687196

Malcolm, W. M., Warwar, S., & Greenberg, L. (2005). Facilitating forgiveness in individual therapy as an approach to resolving interpersonal injuries. In E. L. Worthington, Jr. (Ed.), *Forgiveness: Theory, research and practice* (pp. 179–202). New York, NY: Guilford.

McAdams, D. P. (2006). *The redemptive self: Stories Americans live by*. New York, NY: Oxford University Press.

Mount, S. D., & Moas, S. (2015). Re-purposing the "empty nest". *Journal of Family Psychology, 26*(3), 247–252.

Paré, D., Young, K., Freedman, J., Scott, T. A., & Behan, C. (2006). Unpacking the "Healing" metaphor: A panel discussion. *Journal of Systemic Therapies, 25*(1), 68–83. doi:10.1521/jsyt.2006.25.1.68

Pondy, L. R. (1983). The role of metaphors and myths in organization and in the facilitation of change. In L. Pondy, P. Fronst, G. Morgan, & T. Dandridge (Eds.), *Organizational symbolism* (pp. 157–166). Greenwich, CT: JAI Press.

Smith, R. C., & Eisenberg, E. (1987). Conflict at Disneyland: A root metaphor analysis. *Communication Monographs, 54*, 367–380.

Turnage, A. (2013). Technological resistance: A metaphor analysis of Enron e-mail messages. *Communication Quarterly, 61*, 519–538.

Waldron, V. (2017). *Middle years of marriage: Challenge, change, and growth*. New York, NY: Peter Lang.

Waldron, V., & Kassing, J. (2017). *Negotiating work relationships*. San Diego, CA: Cognella Publishing.

Waldron, V. R., & Kelley, D. L. (2008). *Communicating forgiveness*. Thousand Oaks, CA: Sage.

Weil, A. (1995). *Spontaneous healing: How to discover and enhance your body's natural ability to maintain and heal itself*. New York, NY: Fawcett Columbine.

PART II

Imaginative Work

Preparing for Change

3

WHEN THINGS GO "WRONG"

Catalysts for Relational Change

My sister and I had a party when we were in high school. Our parents were out of town, so we saw it as a prime opportunity. We had been planning it for a couple of weeks. Everyone knew about it. Well, over a hundred people showed up! Anyway, it turned out that a chair caught on fire, someone stole our Dustbuster (don't ask!), and some tile in the family room was broken. Needless to say, when my parents got home the %x#@ hit the fan! Of course, my sister and I cried and told them it wasn't supposed to be that big. We told them how sorry we were and that it would never happen again. They were mad at us (understandable), but they forgave us. They said they understood we were young and things are going to happen, but it didn't excuse what we had done. They pointed out all the repercussions that could have come along with our stupidity. Considering what we had done, it was pretty good of them to forgive us. That was eight years ago. Now we laugh about it. We told them that we actually planned the party – our relationship is still great. – Jen, age 25 (Waldron & Kelley, 2008, pp. 91, 92)

★

Jen's story may be all too familiar (she's not one of our kids, but certainly could be!). Indeed, many parents have experienced the disappointment that accompanies a child's decision to violate a trust or place themselves or others at risk. And, many children look back on decisions they've made with complex thoughts and emotions. Jen's parents seem to have handled the situation with relative calm and some imagination, reframing their daughter's behavior from a willful violation of family rules to a "teachable moment". Their firm but forgiving response is one reason, at least in Jen's mind, that the parent–offspring relationship remains "great". In fact, telling stories of overcoming adversity is one way that families and couples become, and stay, resilient (Buzzanell, 2018; Socha & Torres, 2015). Although it has taken years to fully unfold, this family story ends with an honest accounting of the past. As we argued in 2008, forgiveness episodes of this kind function to express and solidify the values and moral commitments that form the foundation of personal relationships (Waldron & Kelley, 2008). In the end, due to the imaginative responses of Jen's parents, what went wrong turned out alright.

Scholars of relational resilience contend that social bonds sometimes become stronger, not weaker, in response to adversity (Zautra, 2013). Resilient families and couples may recognize that familiar patterns are no longer working, and they reorganize their relationships in response (Waldron, 2017). The purpose of this chapter is to identify what might not be working, what might feel "wrong" in personal relationships. It develops a theme first introduced in *Chapter 1*, that the disappointments and disruptions of life are often the catalyst for relational reimagination. The proverbial "wake-up call" is a familiar example, the unfortunate event that finally prompts a person to face reality and make some long overdue changes to a floundering marriage or a toxic friendship. In this spirit, the present chapter helps the reader identify three kinds of adversity that can prompt relationship change. Then it considers three creative communicative responses to adversity (talking resilience into being, rebooting moral conversations, and sharing stories of redemption), all of which lay the groundwork for constructive change.

So, Where Did Things Go Wrong? Three Types of Relational Adversity

As we navigate the landscape of what went wrong, we visit three distinct regions. First is the realm of relational transgressions, those seemingly intentional acts that cause hurt and harm. In some cases, transgressions are violations of relationship rules – the explicit or implied agreements that govern the interactions of couples, friends, and family members (Metts, 1994; Metts & Asbury, 2015). Some of these are handled routinely. Unintended and ordinary, they include fleeting acts of inattention or thoughtlessness that can often be addressed with a quick "Oh, I'm sorry" or "That came out wrong . . . Let me say it a different way". Yet even these seemingly benign violations can signal a need for relationship change, especially if they become chronic (Beck, 2017). Indeed, if left unaddressed, niggling feelings of irritation can fester and mutate into a toxic and exasperating relational rash, one that must be diagnosed and treated by those involved, possibly with the aid of a professional.

Second, we cover the ground of relational trauma (Harvey, 2004; Waldron & Kelley, 2008). Here we consider the actions of family members, lovers, and friends that cause deep and widespread relational injury, even when harm was unintended. Our tour of this variety of "wrong" is defined by two landmarks. First, the injury is "relational" rather than simply individual. For example, whole families can be traumatized when a sibling is incarcerated, a teenager becomes addicted, or a parent engages in reckless financial behavior. The second landmark is the unintended consequences of the harmful act. The harm caused by the actor is accidental, attributable to recklessness, an unforeseen consequence of a partner's behavior.

Third, we navigate the terrain of relational stressors, disruptions that "just happen" as partners grow in age and experience, life events force them to adjust, and the world around them changes in unexpected or unpleasant ways (Waldron, 2017). To illustrate, consider how spouses adjust as their aging bodies affect sexual response, how siblings respond to the death of a parent, how children and step-parents react to new family arrangements, how whole families are affected by an economic downturn that reduces their income. When things go wrong in these ways, it is hard to lay the blame. No one individual is at fault. And yet, these events can feel "wrong" and motivate relationship change.

That Really Hurt! Transgressions as Catalysts for Change

We define a transgression as a deliberate and harmful act performed by one or more partners in a relationship. Our interviews with romantic partners aged 18 to 90 years tell us that even the longest and most loving relationships have weathered serious adversity, including hurtful acts initiated by family members and partners (Kelley, 2014; Waldron, 2017; Waldron & Kelley, 2008, 2009). Of course, there are exceptions. A few couples described a blissful and unruffled romantic journey and some families reported few of these challenges. But for most, relational life includes some unexpected and unpleasant surprises. The sibling who refused to pitch-in when mom or dad got sick and needed help. The promising relationship that was quashed by the discovery that your girlfriend slept with another guy. The coworker who took credit for the good work you performed. The trusted friend who failed to keep your darkest secret a secret. The parent who seemed to favor your sister over you. The son who ended up in jail.

This chapter addresses both chronic and acute transgressions, but it focuses on those that are serious from the get go, the ones that leave people feeling shocked, wounded, deeply disappointed, wronged, fearful, or angry. In addition, we explore a variety of factors that influence how we experience transgressions.

Types of transgressions

Researcher Sandra Metts has delved deeply into the nature of transgressions, linking them closely with violations of relational rules (Metts, 1994; Metts & Asbury, 2015). With other scholars (e.g., Merolla, 2017) we reserve the term "transgression" for acts that are serious enough to require forgiveness. Harvey's (2004) analysis of transgressions, reported by romantic partners in our studies, identified acts of verbal aggression, expressions of extreme anger, public embarrassments, betrayals, unilateral decision-making, and infidelity, among other acts. Although these transgressions appear to be quite different, experience tells us they can be "boiled down" to three fundamental problems.

First, some of these acts convey disrespect for the partner and attack his or her identity. Behaviors such as being rude in public or making insults imply that the other party is inferior, devalued, incompetent, and undeserving of equal treatment. Vangelisti (1994) has conducted an impressive line of research on "messages that hurt". In several studies, she asked undergraduates to describe "a situation in which someone said something that hurt their feelings" (p. 60). Accusations ("you are such a liar") and threats ("if I find out you are ever with that person, never come home again") were among the types of hurtful messages she reported.

Second, some transgressions violate important relational agreements (Hargrave, 1994). Although not always made explicit, relationships are governed by expectations about such matters as mutual caring, trust, loyalty, collaborative decision making, confidentiality, and honesty, among others. As Metts (2004) indicates, some of these values are encoded as informal rules. For example, "no flirting with others" is a common prohibition in romantic relationships. A young woman shared a different rule that had developed in her marriage:

> While fighting one day, my husband called me stupid. I was so astounded and hurt, I simply closed the door and left. Later we talked about it and he explained his stress and the fact that he did not mean it. I forgave him, but explained that certain things simply shouldn't be said, because I could not forget. "No name calling" has become a rule in our relationship and we stand by it. It's helped us fight fairly.
>
> (Waldron & Kelley, 2008, p. 30)

In more recent studies of friends, Vangelisti has identified the keeping of secrets as a relational rule (e.g., Vangelisti & Nelson, 2015). She notes that friends risk serious relationship rupture if they violate confidences, unless there is a morally justified reason for doing so (e.g., keeping the secret is a safety risk for one of the parties).

The third general type of transgression involves acts of injustice. Vince has studied these in the workplace, finding that they involve perceived abuses of power, unjust rewards and excessive punishments, and favoritism (Waldron, 2000). After reviewing the reports from numerous blue- and white-collar workers, he found that transgressions are compounded when the power difference between the offender and victim is substantial, there exists an audience of peers, and the victim believes she or he is being targeted despite acting in the best interests of the organization (as opposed to self-interest). Doug has examined the language of injustice as it appears in the talk of romantic partners, finding that the tenor of a marriage is shaped by discourses of inequity, lack of respect, and processes that undermine equal participation (Kelley, 2015).

Assessing the damage: How big of a deal is this?

Not all transgressions are created equal. Some have acute and serious ramifications, far more serious than the purloined Dustbuster reported by Jen in the opening vignette. These acts cause real injury, usually psychological but sometimes physical, to people and the relationships that bind them. And if we know anything from the research, it is that the more serious the transgression, the more communicative effort will be needed to heal the relationship (Merolla, 2017; Scobie & Scobie, 1998). What makes a transgression more or less serious? Well, that is partly a subjective judgment, grounded in the expectations of the partners and assessments of how far a violation goes in breaching relationship agreements. Still, previous scholarship gives us some ideas to work with.

"I just can't get past that!": Unforgivable acts. Drawing on deeply held views shaped by family socialization, religion, and culture, some of our research participants find certain acts to be simply "unforgivable" (Kelley, 1998). For them, once these acts are performed the transgressor must be rejected and, typically, the relationship is viewed as irreparable. "That is where I draw the line. I just couldn't stay with him if he had sex with someone else. I don't see how anyone could. It's just not part of my moral code. Forget it!" These sentiments, expressed by one of our younger students, underscore the fact that a person's moral sensibility can make some relational transgressions seem truly unforgivable (Backman, 1985). Our student was commenting on the most frequently mentioned unforgivable offense in romantic relationships (at least in our studies): Infidelity. Some older couples shared this sentiment, too. Margaret (in her mid-60s) noted first, "We were brought up that you try to stay with your husband no matter what." Then she added, "But I think if Asa had wandered off or something, I would have probably been out of here. You know that?" (Waldron & Kelley, 2008, p. 34).

What one family or couple considers unforgivable, another will shrug off. Indeed, some couples negotiate open relationships in which extramarital sex is unproblematic. Importantly, the definition of "unforgiveable" may evolve as individuals and relationships progress through the lifecourse, relational investment grows, and perspectives change. We find that some even come to view infidelity to be forgivable. Jan wanted to at least try to preserve her investment in a long-term relationship:

> Are we willing to throw away 32 years, you know, just for a fling? I take it seriously; it crushed me. And it's probably changed me a lot, but I still don't know that I want to be alone and give up what we have, even though the marriage was on real shaky ground there for a while. So we went through a couple of years of crap. Are we going to throw away 32 years because of it? If you're not willing to work through the hard times, you're just not going to make it.
>
> (Waldron & Kelley, 2008, p. 34)

In our research, participants have described other transgressions they consider to be potentially unforgivable, such as physical violence, changes in sexual identity, drug abuse, neglectful parenting, and certain criminal acts. And yet, we find that some participants come to change their views, to rethink their assumptions. Due to his own family experience (recounted in *Chapter 1*), Vince sometimes speaks with parents of transgender persons. For some, particularly those from traditional religious backgrounds, the decision to alter one's gender identification is morally unsettling, a transgression against the "natural order" of things determined by God. And yet, many such parents come to think differently as they learn more about the courageous journey taken by those who have dared to embrace their true gender identity.

"You did that on purpose!": Intent. Attribution theorists (e.g., Weiner, 1996) have long argued that our reactions to offenses are calibrated by our understanding of their cause. For example, if we view a transgression to be intentional, the result of the offender's free will, we are likely to judge it as more serious than an offense that can be explained as an "accident" or the result of external forces that the offender could not fully control. Manusov (2015) reminds us that we often make these attributions without much awareness. And as she notes, our attributions can be quite faulty. They tend to be influenced by experiences from the past ("He is just being lazy again") and often are made without a full consideration of current circumstances. In this sense, the attribution process at times can seem to be efficient, but really be self-serving. In contrast, Manusov suggests that mindfulness may help relational parties be fully present, open-minded, and inquisitive with one another.

"I think I was just dissed": Face threats. According to theorists working in the identity management tradition, face is the self-identity that persons value and want others to affirm (Goffman, 1959). When a partner commits a face-threatening act, he or she may be expected to repair the relationship by seeking forgiveness (Merolla, 2017). Depending on the relational context, a person might value their identity as a compassionate friend, loving parent, competent employee, or hardworking student. Because people are highly invested in these self-conceptions, actions that threaten face often produce deep emotional reactions. For example, the experience of being criticized in front of one's peers is among the most emotionally disturbing experiences reported by employees (Waldron, 2009). The presence of an audience makes these face-threatening experiences even more unpleasant, as the magnitude of the violation expands with the number of persons with whom the victim would have to perform identity "repair work". For that reason, an act such as infidelity might become more serious when the offense is known by members of a couple's social network. Afifi, Falato, and Weiner (2001), drawing in part from the work of Goffman, reason that highly face-threatening acts may be more difficult to forgive. So, serious transgressions may be those that are experienced as deeply face-threatening.

"I thought we had an agreement": Relational covenant. Relationships are typically governed by certain rules of decorum, such as family prohibitions on a child's use of certain forms of slang or an agreement by long-distance friends to "check-in" once a month. But some relational agreements run deeper. These are fundamental to the identity of the relationship and may even feel "sacred" to the participants, a kind of relational covenant (Hargrave, 2004). Violations of these can be "deal breakers". Guerrero and her colleagues (e.g., Guerrero & Cole, 2015) have examined violations of four fundamental relational standards in dating relationships, finding that we expect our romantic interests to exhibit caring, fidelity (loyalty), honesty, and respect for our own autonomy. Violations of these result in intense emotional reactions that the researchers clustered under the themes of *anger* (e.g., frustrated, resentful), *vulnerable* (e.g., disappointed, sad), *distress* (e.g., anxious, fearful), *embarrassed* (e.g., humiliated, shame), and *shock* (e.g., shock, surprise). Among dating couples, these emotions are catalysts for destructive and defensive behavioral responses such as relational distancing, combative conflict, and revenge. For example, responses to partners who exhibited reasonable jealousy (a controlling behavior classified as an autonomy violation) included feelings of distress and vulnerability and, sometimes, efforts to create emotional distance between the partners.

Autocratic decision making (a violation of the autonomy standard) is a fairly common theme in the forgiveness episodes we have studied. For example, Judy and Dion had been married for 15 years when he decided unilaterally to move the family from Pennsylvania to Mississippi (see Waldron & Kelley, 2008, p. 30). To this day, Judy isn't sure she completely forgives him. There were plenty of things for Judy to be frustrated about: Loss of friends, the complications of moving, being near in-laws. But the key transgression was this: "We didn't share the decision. And I think that's the biggest thing with relationships. You must share in decisions. You can't have one that just dominates." As Judy's words suggest, violations of key covenants prompt relational rethinking, and in some cases, the effects are long lasting.

"I will forgive you if . . .": Staying safe. In her analysis of the relational acts that require forgiveness, Dayna realized that certain kinds of transgressions appeared more likely to be forgiven conditionally (Kloeber, 2011; Kloeber & Waldron, 2017). That is, the victimized party imposed stipulations as a prerequisite for forgiveness, such as "I will forgive you, but only if you get help". In this way, conditional forgiveness is an act of relationship reimagination because it proposes a future in which at least one of the partners will be adopting new relational responsibilities. As a group, these transgressions involve fundamental threats to the safety of the relationship or the offended partner's ability to predict relational outcomes. One such transgression involves the repeated abuse of substances. In such cases, transgressors are viewed as unsafe or unpredictable. For example, in Dayna's study a mother considered her husband an unsafe father when he was drinking around the children. In contrast to unconditional forgiveness, the conditional type offers a degree of protection against recurrent transgressions and, perhaps, a rationale for an exit from the relationship by the vulnerable party if safety is not restored.

"It's my fault too": Mutual offenses. When discussing transgressions, researchers often invoke the terms "victims" and "offenders", but theorists recognize that the responsibility for transgressions is often shared, even when one party is mostly to blame (Exline & Baumeister, 2000). Expressions of anger are frequently reciprocal, even though started by one party. Hostile behavior sometimes arises from a mutual failure to address simmering differences. Defensiveness typically breeds defensiveness. In Harvey's (2004) analysis of transgressions reported in our early studies of forgiveness (Waldron & Kelley, 2008), some couples described personality differences as a triggering condition for forgiveness episodes. For these couples, a mismatch on such personality features as extroversion/introversion or emotionality led to persistent conflicts and occasional blow-outs. These examples support the perspective that transgressions often arise from interaction between parties, not just the actions of an individual transgressor. They may feel severe, generating a sense of hopelessness, because personality attributes seem fixed, unchanging. In these situations relationship imagination can be especially useful as a mutual process, rather than individual adjustment.

"You're driving me nuts": Bad habits and blowouts. In sharing stories of forgiveness, couples sometimes tell us that a pattern of mild transgression builds to serious moments of truth. One husband described how a persistent pattern led to a major blowup:

> And it led back to the fact that I was leaving my socks around. I mean, it's just something so stupid, minor, but you keep bringing it up and bringing it up and bringing it up and it becomes major, you know.
>
> (Waldron & Kelley, 2008, p. 33)

Simmering resentments sometimes become volatile, as Rose (in her mid-60s) related in this story about her marriage with Jim, who in the early days of their marriage was frequently more focused on his work than on her emotional needs. After repeatedly taking second place to Jim's work, Rose exploded:

> He just made me mad. Whatever difficulties he had had that day at work, he brought them home and I was cooking, and I was happy. Then he said something that upset me and I just . . . I had a knife in my hand and just turned and threw it at him! He looked and went out the door, went to the store, came back in, put his beer in the refrigerator and we sat down for dinner. We didn't say very much. Then we went to bed and the next morning we got up and he says, "I'm sorry."
>
> (Waldron & Kelley, 2008, p. 33)

For Rose, the point seemed to be that her husband's obsession with his own concerns finally drove her to the brink. Jim must have recognized this, as he offered an apology (and apparently decided against pressing charges!). The couple saw this incident as a "wakeup call". It clearly illustrates that relationship-changing transgressions needn't be fully intentional and they needn't be discrete events. They can unfold over long periods of time. In fact, some transgressions are viewed more as bad habits or patterns of harmful behavior. Overreliance on alcohol and other substances, long periods of moodiness, and habitual inconsiderateness were all described by our research participants as forms of behavior that triggered a relationship-changing conflict.

Relationally Traumatizing Experiences: Unintended Harm and Relationship Reimagination

Thus far we have assumed that transgressions are intentional and harmful. However, many injurious acts are performed unintentionally, or at least partly so (Scobie & Scobie, 1998). And some deeply painful experiences are attributable to recklessness, ignorance, prejudice, and accidents. We will call these relationally traumatizing experiences (RTEs). Although it may not be clear who to blame, partners, families, and friends are left feeling hurt, bewildered, or resentful – often the target of one another's pain. As Harvey's (2004) investigation makes clear, victims of traumatic relational experiences often expect the actors to take responsibility and seek atonement ("make up for") for the damage their actions caused. Vince and his colleagues recently reported a taxonomy of the relational challenges reported by 265 middle-aged couples (Waldron, Przytula Vynalek, Cayetano, Kloeber, & Tuholsky, 2017, p. 54). Several of them were of the type we have labeled relationship-traumatizing. They reported, for example, that some spouses were deeply affected by their partners' bad financial decisions, unwillingness to seek appropriate mental health counseling, or drug abuse. As parents, participants were sometimes traumatized when adult offspring failed as a mother or father, committed a serious crime, or chose to relocate far away from family. In no case were the actions intended to harm the participants, but nonetheless, they reported great pain. Often spouses or offspring were held responsible for this unintended trauma. Rounds of accusation, defensiveness, and hostility opened breaches in these relationships. These behaviors in themselves can be traumatic, making it more likely that the parties will rethink their relationship and (perhaps) need assistance in healing from the trauma (for example, see Waldron & Kelley, 2008).

Vince's work on midlife trauma indicates that relational partners are capable of bouncing back from such adversity, by recalibrating their expectations and reimagining the roles they might play in a new future. One example was reported by Lupe', who told the story of her "shattered" parents' response to her unwed sister's pregnancy:

. . . my sister who was their "baby" got pregnant, and it shattered their world. They didn't know how to cope with it; they felt they had failed as parents. Their dream for us was to walk out of our house dressed in white the day of our wedding, and now that dream wouldn't come true. My parents were extremely disappointed; they wouldn't talk to my sister and were forcing her to marry the guy. However, once my nephew was born, it completely changed their world and they now see it as a blessing. This baby brought a new joy to my parent's lives; they love the role of being traditional grandparents. . . . They feel that this baby has given them a new light, since their kids are grown this baby is able to fill that void and give them something to look forward to.

*&%# Happens: Life Course Events Spur Relationship Change

Another way relationships go wrong involves disruptive lifecourse events. Early theorists of adult development, such as Duvall (1977), Erikson (1959), and Levinson (Levinson, 1996; Levinson, Darrow, Klein, Levinson, & McKee, 1978), charted the challenges and opportunities encountered at various stages of life. Some of these are familiar to younger readers, such as the difficulties that arise for (some) parents when adult offspring leave behind an "empty nest" (Bouchard, 2014). Having grown comfortable in the identity of "parent", spouses may feel a sense of loss and confusion when their children no longer need active parenting. However, in many cases the parent–child relationship is successfully reimagined (Waldron, 2017).

A recent study of stepchild–stepparent relationships (Braithwaite et al., 2018) found that the dissolution of the original family was a highly disruptive lifecourse event. However, in strong stepfamily relationships, this adversity was managed by adapting some family routines and adopting some new ones. For example, stepparents were invited to participate in familiar family rituals, such as Christmas celebrations. But new forms of celebration were also added to stepfamily family routines.

Later in the lifecourse, certain forms of adversity are more common. We found that older spouses sometimes struggled with the effects of retirement on their incomes and identities (Waldron & Kelley, 2009). Late in life, when serious illness is more common, spouses and their families may find themselves adapting to new caregiving roles. We also found, for example, that men used to traditional masculine roles learned to become caregivers for their ailing wives, another example of relationship reimagination spurred by lifecourse events.

All of this is to say that in relationships, things go wrong in a variety of ways, some intended, some not; some expected, some not so much. Yet, in all of the cases described above, adversity creates the opportunity for creative adaptation. Later in this book, we consider several powerful processes of relationship imagination, including those of forgiveness and reconciliation. Here we offer a few communication practices that may help relationship partners, be they romantic, family, or friends, adapt in the face of adversity.

Making Change: Creative Communicative Responses to Adversity

Although transgressions, traumatizing experiences, and unsettling life events are inevitably painful, we do find inspiration in the stories from our students, research participants, and ourselves that demonstrate the ability to thrive in the face of adversity. Clinicians and researchers have identified processes that help people adapt and cope during relationship disruption. Adversity can be the catalyst for change that eventually makes us healthier and happier. Below we identify several forms of what might be called creative relational communication.

Talking Relational Resilience "Into Being"

Buzzanell and her colleagues (Buzzanell, 2010, 2018) have studied resilience in relationships disrupted by economic misfortune and other traumatic experiences. A much-studied concept in recent decades, resilience is a system's capacity to recover, normalize, and even thrive after serious disruption (for a review, see Reich, Zautra, & Hall, 2010). Significantly, human resilience often engages imagination in that systems must adapt, find ways to normalize, and use metaphorical language to manage relationship upheaval. In this chapter, we have documented many sources of "relational disruption", ranging from marital infidelity to job loss. Buzzanell's research identified several important discourse practices that families use to literally talk resilience "into being" when they are faced with economic hardship (Lucas & Buzzanell, 2012). For example, in interactions with their children, parents tended to acknowledge their negative emotions but foregrounded the *actions* the family could take to control its fate. In this way parents might acknowledge that children were disappointed in what would be a meager Christmas, but emphasize the fun the children would have in the process of handmaking gifts for siblings and friends. These families also retained "normal" patterns of behavior as much as possible, often by both preserving and adjusting familiar routines. For example, a family who could no longer afford to go out for dinner on Friday night would continue to "go out", but they would pack a picnic basket instead. The researchers also found numerous examples of figurative language that communicated a family was prepared for hardship – able for instance to *tighten the belt*, find *sidelines* (alternative sources of income), and *make ends meet*.

Vince's report on resilience in 265 midlife couples identified "resilience-enhancing" practices as well underlying "root" metaphors that guided couples as they navigated trying times (Waldron, 2017). Practices included "broadening the base" of a couple's social connections in order to cultivate badly needed support. Many of them had spent years supporting their children and friends. Faced with serious adversity, they learned to ask others (including adult offspring) for advice, emotional support, and even financial help. Other helpful practices included "reestablishing solidarity" (emphasizing shared goals, speaking in one voice) and "recalibrating expectations" (reducing disappointment by accepting more realistic views of self, partner, and the future). Resilience was also cultivated by the metaphors couples used to describe themselves. Faced with serious adversity such as a diagnosis of cancer or job loss, these couples described themselves as "battlers" and "survivors" tested by war. They characterized the relationship as a "marathon, not a sprint", having recognized the importance of patience, endurance, and the preservation of resources. They spoke of adversity as an opportunity to "fine tune" a valued relationship that was temporarily sputtering, perhaps due to poor "maintenance" practices. And some couples portrayed themselves as realists. Rather than avoiding adversity, these learned to "deal with it", "hash things out", and "put your cards on the table".

Rebooting Moral Conversations

After years of listening to couples and families talk about their responses to transgressions, we started thinking of these conversations as "moral negotiations" (Waldron & Kelley, 2008, 2018). This idea came to us because so many people used moral terms when they described what went wrong and how the relationship should change. "It was just so *wrong*", a confidant might say about the treatment of a tyrannical boss. "It's just not *right*", we heard, for a friend to reveal a sensitive secret, for a partner to lie about his past, for an adult son to be so dismissive of his parents' concerns. While all these statements express disappointment, sometimes even outrage, they serve a very important function of voicing the values that matter most to the speaker. Sometimes these are values that the speaker assumes are shared by others. But, in speaking them, they create the opportunity to test that assumption, to hear how others view things, to determine whether the violation they perceive to be so serious is less so in the minds of their friends, family members, and even those who committed the offense.

Discussions of offenses are "negotiations" in the sense that the parties express their own values and, sometimes, develop a better understanding of those held by others. We don't mean that the parties compromise their values to make peace. Instead, they interrogate values, review their origins in family and cultural socialization, recommit to those that hold up under scrutiny, and hold self and other accountable for violations of those relational standards. Ultimately, this process may lead them to reimagine a relationship that feels "good", to be more willing to release their anger and replace it with a renewed sense of confidence in the relationship's future. Or, the parties may come to realize that the relationship they had enjoyed was simply untested, grounded in illusions rather than realities.

In such cases it might be better to change the relationship or abandon it altogether. It may be time to seek a better boss or to date a more trustworthy girlfriend. In either case, the unfortunate and painful transgression prompts relational rethinking and, sometimes, solidifies the moral commitments that undergird relationships that are good, in the moral sense of that word.

Creating Stories of Redemption

Scholars such as McAdams and colleagues (McAdams, 2013, 2014) have looked to the art of storytelling for evidence of how people overcome difficult experiences in their lives, including the serious mistakes they have made and the transgressions that have been committed against them. It turns out that most people have experienced these adversities. And yet, McAdams has found differences in the stories that people tell about these experiences. It appears that redemptive storytellers construct life narratives that leave them feeling more satisfied with life and more generous ("generative") toward others. In particular, "redemptive" narratives highlight the advantages the storyteller has experienced (e.g., dumb luck; the help of a generous boss; a parent who stuck by them) in addition to the challenges. They communicate an awareness, perhaps grounded in personal experience, that *many* other people also experience undeserved suffering, inequality, and oppression. These stories share the moral framework that eventually guides the storyteller through difficult times ("I stayed focused on my family" or "I learned to be honest with myself"). Finally, these stories include *redemptive* sequences – episodes in which seemingly negative experiences result in positive outcomes, such as lessons learned or unexpected opportunity ("I hated the job, but showed up on time every day, and the owner of the business finally recognized my potential"). These redemptive storytellers also express a desire to use their experiences for positive social goals, such as helping others succeed.

Partners and family members may find it helpful to jointly construct stories of redemption in the wake of hard times. These stories become problem-solving resources in the sense that they yield lessons from the past that could be helpful now, to the teller and to those with whom he or she interacts (Beck, 2017; Socha & Torres, 2015). Also, the positive emotions created by these stories can counter some of the anger or distress that people feel after transgressions and other disruptive events, perhaps making negative rumination less likely. And, by cooperating to construct stories of the past, family members and other partners generate goodwill and rebuild connections that may have been frayed by adversity.

Catalysts for Relationship Change

The three communicative practices reviewed at the end of this chapter – resilience enhancing communication, moral conversations, and redemptive storytelling – embody the theme of this book as they demonstrate that persons, couples, and families can respond creatively and constructively to transgressions, relationship-traumatizing events, and life disruptions. In these ways, adversity is reinterpreted as a potential catalyst that may yield new relational practices even as marriages, families, and friendships are preserved. Although preliminary, the research suggests that some of these practices are even transmitted across generations, as adult offspring reproduce resilient practices modeled by parents and other elders (Lucas & Buzzanell, 2012). Of course, we recognize that change is seldom easy and, as Chapter 4 suggests, when things do go "wrong" our emotions play a significant role.

References

Afifi, W. A., Falato, W. L., & Weiner, J. L. (2001). Identity concerns following a severe relational transgression: The role of discovery method for the relational outcomes of infidelity. *Journal of Social and Personal Relationships, 18,* 291–308.

Backman, C. W. (1985). Identity, self-presentation, and the resolution of moral dilemmas: Towards a social psychological theory of moral behavior. In B. R. Schlenker (Ed.), *The self and social life* (pp. 261–289). New York, NY: McGraw-Hill.

Beck, G. A. (2017). Theorizing relational resilience at midlife. In V. Waldron (Ed.), *The middle years of marriage: Challenge, change, and growth* (pp. 143–164). New York, NY: Peter Lang.

Bouchard, G. (2014). How do parents react when their children leave home? An integrative review. *Journal of Adult Development, 21,* 69–79.

Braithwaite, D. O., Waldron, V. R., Allen, J., Oliver, B., Bergquist, G., Brockhage, K., . . . Tschampl-Diesing, C. (2018). "Feeling warmth and close to her": Communication and Resilience Reflected in Turning Points in Positive Adult Stepchild–Stepparent Relationships. *Journal of Family Communication, 18,* 92–109.

Buzzanell, P. M. (2010). Resilience: Talking, resisting, and imagining new normalcies into being. *Journal of Communication, 60,* 1–14.

Buzzanell, P. M. (2018). Organizing resilience as adaptive-transformational tensions. *Journal of Applied Communication Research, 46*(1), 14–18. doi:10.1080/00909882.2018. 1426711

Duvall, E. R. (1977). *Marriage and family development*. Philadelphia. PA: Lippincott Williams & Wilkins.

Erikson, E. H. (1959). *Identity and the life cycle*. New York, NY: International Universities Press.

Exline, J. J., & Baumeister, R. F. (2000). Expressing forgiveness and repentance: Benefits and barriers. In M. C. McCullough, K. I. Pargament, & C. E. Thoresen (Eds.), *Forgiveness: Theory, research, and practice* (pp. 133–155). New York, NY: Guilford.

Goffman, E. (1959). *The presentation of self in everyday life*. Garden City, NY: Doubleday.

Guerrero, L. K., & Cole, M. (2015). Moral standards, emotions, and communication associated with relational transgressions in dating relationships. In V. R. Waldron & D. L. Kelley (Eds.), *Moral talk across the lifespan: Creating good relationships* (pp. 155–182). New York, NY: Peter Lang.

Hargrave, T. D. (1994). Families and forgiveness. A theoretical and therapeutic perspective. *The Family Journal: Counseling and Therapy for Couples and Families, 2,* 339–348.

Harvey, J. (2004). *Trauma and recovery strategies across the lifespan of long-term married couples.* Phoenix: Arizona State University West Press.

Kelley, D. L. (1998). The communication of forgiveness. *Communication Studies, 49,* 255–271.

Kelley, D. L. (2015). Chapter 4: Just relationships. In V. R. Waldron & D. L. Kelley (Eds.), *Moral talk across the lifespan: Creating good relationships* (pp. 75–94). New York, NY: Peter Lang.

Kloeber, D. N. (2011). Voicing conditional forgiveness. Arizona State University.

Kloeber, D. N., & Waldron, V. R. (2017). Expressing and suppressing conditional forgiveness in serious romantic relationships. In J. Samp (Ed.), *Communicating interpersonal conflict in close relationships: Contexts, challenges, and opportunities* (pp. 227–249). New York, NY: Routledge.

Levinson, D. (1996). *The seasons of a woman's life.* New York, NY: Random House.

Levinson, D., Darrow, C. N., Klein, E. B., Levinson, M., & McKee, B. (1978). *The seasons of a man's life.* New York, NY: Knopf.

Lucas, K., & Buzzanell, P. M. (2012). Memorable messages of hard times: Constructing short- and long-term resiliencies through family communication. *Journal of Family Communication, 12*(3), 189–208. doi:10.1080/15267431.2012.687196

Manusov, V. (2015). Mindfulness as morality: Awareness, nonjudgment, and non-reactivity in couples' communication. In V. Waldron & D. Kelley (Eds.), *Developing good relationships: Moral communication across the lifespan* (pp. 183–201). New York, NY: Peter Lang.

McAdams, D. P. (2013). *The redemptive self: Stories Americans live by* (Rev. ed.). New York, NY: Oxford University Press.

McAdams, D. P. (2014). The life narrative at midlife. *New Directions for Child and Adolescent Development, 145,* 57–69. doi:10.1002/cad.20067

Merolla, A. J. (2017). Forgiveness following conflict: What it is, why it happens, and how it's done. In J. A. Samp (Ed.), *Communicating interpersonal conflict in close relationships: Contexts, challenges, and opportunities* (pp. 227–249). New York, NY: Routledge.

Metts, S. (1994). Relational transgressions. In W. R. Cupach & B. H. Spitzberg (Eds.), *The dark side of interpersonal communication* (pp. 217–241). Hillsdale, NJ: Lawrence Erlbaum.

Metts, S. (2004). First sexual involvement in romantic relationships: An empirical investigation of communicative framing, romantic beliefs and attachment orientation in the passion turning point. In J. H. Harvey, A. Wenzel, & S. Sprecher (Eds.), *The handbook of sexuality in close relationships* (pp. 135–158). Mahwah, NJ: Lawrence Erlbaum Associates.

Metts, S., & Asbury, B. (2015). Unfolding the transgression scene. In G. A. Beck & T. J. Socha (Eds.), *Communicating hope and resilience across the lifespan* (pp. 75–94). New York, NY: Peter Lang.

Reich, J., Zautra, A., & Hall, J. (2010). *Handbook of adult resilience.* New York, NY: Guilford.

Scobie, E. D., & Scobie, G. E. W. (1998). Damaging events: The perceived need for forgiveness. *Journal for the Theory of Social Behavior, 28,* 373–401.

Socha, T. J., & Torres, A. (2015). Life's "war stories": Accounts of resilience and hope. In G. A. Beck & T. J. Socha (Eds.), *Communicating hope and resilience across the lifespan* (pp. 219–234). New York, NY: Peter Lang.

Vangelisti, A. (1994). Messages that hurt. In W. R. Cupach & B. H. Spitzberg (Eds.), *The dark side of interpersonal communication* (pp. 53–82). Hillsdale, NJ: Lawrence Erlbaum.

Vangelisti, A. L., & Nelson, E. C. (2015). The morality of revealing others' secrets. In V. Waldron & D. Kelley (Eds.), *Developing good relationships: Moral communication across the lifespan* (pp. 137–154). New York, NY: Peter Lang.

Waldron, V. R. (2000). Relational experiences and emotion at work. In S. Fineman (Ed.), *Emotion in organizations* (2nd ed., pp. 64–82). Thousand Oaks, CA: Sage Publications.

Waldron, V. R. (2009). Emotional tyranny at work: Suppressing the moral emotions. In P. Lutgen-Sandvik & B. Davenport-Sypher (Eds.), *Destructive organizational communication: Processes, consequences, and constructive ways of organizing* (pp. 9–26). New York, NY: Routledge.

Waldron, V. (2017). *Middle years of marriage: Challenge, change, and growth.* New York, NY: Peter Lang.

Waldron, V. R., Przytula Vynalek, A., Cayetano, C., Kloeber, D., & Tuholsky, A. (2017). Midlife changes and challenges. Middle years of marriage: Challenge, change, and growth. In V. Waldron (Ed.), *The middle years of marriage: Challenge, change, and growth* (pp. 143–164). New York, NY: Peter Lang.

Waldron, V. R., & Kelley, D. L. (2008). *Communicating forgiveness.* Thousand Oaks, CA: Sage.

Waldron, V. R., & Kelley, D. L. (2009). *Marriage at midlife.* New York, NY: Springer-Verlag.

Waldron, V. R., & Kelley, D. L. (2018). Negotiated morality theory: How family communication shapes our values. In D. O. Braithwaite, E. A. Suter, & K. Floyd (Eds.), *Engaging theories in family communication: Multiple perspectives* (2nd ed., pp. 233–243). New York, NY: Taylor & Francis.

Weiner, B. (1996). Searching for order in social motivation. *Psychological Inquiry, 7*(3), 199–216. doi:10.1207/s15327965pli0703_1

Zautra, A. J. (2013). Resilience is social, after all. In M. Kent, M. C. Davis, & J. W. Reich (Eds.), *Handbook of resilience approaches to stress and trauma* (pp. 185–196). New York, NY: Routledge.

4

EMOTIONAL RESPONSE

Motivation for Relational Change

Karen and Josh had known each other for ten years and been living together for four. They were not "married", but they had signed health powers of attorney for one another and one summer's day had invited friends to journey with them to the mountains where they shared poetry as a celebration of their commitment. However, after a career-related relocation to accommodate Josh's promotion, Karen saw that her soulmate had become preoccupied with work – the beautiful rhythm that had so characterized their love for one another had come to a standstill. Karen's emotions slowly built to a crescendo. Feeling unanchored after the move, Karen sensed that she and Josh were often "out of sync". Thinking about dissolving the relationship, Karen flew back to Albuquerque to talk with a few old friends . . . to get perspective. However, each conversation seemed to Karen as if her friends were defending the "old Josh". In her mind, the old Josh didn't exist any longer.

She experienced a wave of emotions – alienation from Josh, irritation with her friends, fear about the future – that threatened to sweep away the confidence she once felt about the future with the man she thought of as her soulmate. She just couldn't see how the two of them could ever work this out . . . could ever find one another again. One night on the phone with Josh, she told him she wasn't coming back. The more he protested, the more she resisted, until in anger he told her, "Just forget it. I'll be fine without you!" The silence that followed the end of the call confirmed for Karen that the old Josh was gone, and that there was no possibility of building a new future. Josh, on the other hand, woke depressed the next day – how had things gotten to this point? How had he said something so hurtful, so untrue?

★

Karen's emotions signaled that something had "gone wrong" in her relationship with Josh. Well before she could put her feelings into words, she knew that the relationship had changed in unwelcome ways. Later, the heightened emotion of the partners was a catalyst for hurtful and relationship-threatening words, words they came to regret as feelings of anger gave way to a deep sense of loss. This chapter explores the power of emotion to reshape relationships, for better and for worse. As the scenario with Karen and Josh demonstrates, emotion influences how we perceive our partners, our communication behaviors, and, ultimately, the choices we make regarding our relationships. Indeed, when feelings run high, "objective considerations may be outweighed by emotional reactions" (Bembenek, Beilke, & Schroeder, 2007, p. 16).

Studies on emotion are vast, and numerous reviews provide comprehensive perspective on the role of emotion in personal and work relationships (English, Oliver, & Gross, 2013; Feldman Barrett, Lewis, & Haviland-Jones, 2018; Metts, 2018; Waldron, 2012). In this chapter, we focus mainly on emotional experiences and expressions that appear to reshape human connections. Here we bring a communicative perspective that focuses on how the experience of emotion is, or can be, expressed and "talked out" in personal relationships in manners that promote relational transformation, resilience, and, sometimes, healing. We begin with a consideration of some of the social functions emotion serves in personal relationships, then explore how emotional intelligence is closely associated with relationship reimagination. We end by tackling a few emotional issues that influence how we understand emotion in personal relationships.

Stirring the Pot: Communication and Emotion as Relationship Ingredients

Emotions are both reactions to our relationship experiences and the constituent elements that shape those same relationships. Indeed, the fact that our connections to others stimulate emotions is one indicator that these connections really *matter* to us. Routine interactions with strangers, fellow commuters, or store clerks are, with a few exceptions, mostly unemotional. You might find yourself feeling mildly appreciative when a stranger makes room for you on a subway, slightly irritated by a rude store clerk, or a bit bemused as you pass children clowning around on a playground. But all-in-all, these feelings are unmemorable affirmations that life is proceeding pretty much as expected, within the range of behaviors we expect in impersonal encounters with humankind. In this sense, ordinary emotional experience adds a bit of color and interest to the daily broth that is routine interaction, but rarely does it add spice, zest, or intense flavoring. Indeed, ordinary life would quickly exhaust us if every encounter tapped deeply into our emotional resources. Imagine if each casual interchange with a clerk or pedestrian stirred deep emotional responses such as burning resentment, startling surprise, unbridled joy, or a penetrating sense of shame. And yet, some of these more concentrated emotional flavorings do function to enrich, and sometimes spoil, the bubbling stew of relationships that nourishes the lives of lovers, family members, friends, and coworkers.

The Protective Function: Keeping Us Safe

Scholars who study emotion from an evolutionary perspective have long wondered about its role in complex relationships and communities, such as those formed by humans and other obviously social creatures, such as monkeys and elephants (see, for example, Floyd, Dinsmore, & Pavlich, 2018). From this long line of research, roots tracing back to Darwin's (1871, 1872/1998) early observations of animals, it appears that emotion plays a significant role in promoting the survival of individuals and collectives. Fear, for instance, may signal danger (de Becker, 1997), the "something is wrong" feeling that alarmed Karen in the opening vignette. Faced with environmental threats, such as a large beast or potential enemies, our ancestors who listened to the feeling of fear may be those who survived to pass along their genes. The physical experience of fear, rooted in heightened alertness and physiological arousal, readies a potential victim to fight or flee. Moreover, the communication of terror to peers facilitates a collective response, one that may have allowed our ancestors to be more effective in repelling threats than the efforts of any one individual. Fear can play similar roles in contemporary relationships. The experience of fear may signal that a person has been placed at risk of emotional or even physical harm. Heeding that fear can be a protective response and sharing it with others (counselors, family members, trusted friends) may trigger the kind of support that allows one to escape an uncomfortable relationship or reconstruct the relationship in a manner that feels safe.

The survival value of emotional signals extends well beyond those associated with fear. Evolutionary psychologists such as Keltner, the author of *Born to be Good* (2009), have argued that certain more "positive" emotions have survival value too. For example, gentle teasing (a prosocial form of emotion-eliciting communication) is sometimes used to evoke feelings of embarrassment in a person who has been accepted into a new organization or friendship group. In such cases, the feeling of embarrassment signals a kind of vulnerability (think of sheepish smiles and red faces). The group's welcoming response to this emotional display is a signal of acceptance and even emotional bonding. This prosocial function of emotion can be contrasted with verbally aggressive efforts to humiliate another person, an instance in which vulnerability is exploited and used to advantage. The resulting emotion of shame signals unworthiness and disapproval. This can be a devastating experience and many people carry with them a lasting sense of shame that stems from early experiences of rejection (see Bene Brown's well-circulated Ted Talk on that subject; TED, 2012). Whether pro- or anti-social in nature, these kinds of emotional experiences can redefine relationships, making them feel more protective or more threatening.

The Moral Function: Guiding Us to Be Good

People often feel emotion in response to violations or affirmations of the written or unwritten codes that make relationships feel right, worthy, or good, in the moral sense of those words. These "moral emotions" have been the focus of scholarly interest for thousands of years (Aristotle, 2000) and have received recent attention as social scientists have become keenly interested in the social dynamics of good character (Haidt, 2003; Waldron, 2009a; Weiner, 2006) and injustice (de Cremer, 2007; Nussbaum, 2016). The role of anger in response to injustice has been the subject of Martha Nussbaum's (2016) recent philosophical writing, which recognizes anger's potential to embolden those who see oppression and wish to resist. This is another sense in which emotion tells us that something has gone wrong. But ultimately, she views anger as an emotion that is too easily weaponized, the driver of vengeful behavior that ultimately causes harm rather than advancing the well-being of persons and societies.

In the last decade, scholars have conceptualized emotion as a reaction to violations of relational justice (Bembenek et al., 2007). They view anger and retaliatory behavior as responses to procedural injustices that are person (e.g., willful rule-breaking that signals disrespect), and interaction focused (e.g., treating one with disrespect). Likewise, disappointment is a primary emotional response when parties to a decision are denied a voice in the process, a particular kind procedural justice violation. Related research by Guerrero and Cole (2015) examines moral standards in personal relationships, and emotional responses to violations of those standards. They found fidelity violations were associated with anger, vulnerability, shock, and embarrassment; honesty violations with vulnerability, shock, and distress; care violations with vulnerability, distress, and anger; and autonomy violations with vulnerability and distress.

In addition to the behaviors of others, actions of the self can stimulate deep emotional responses. Guilt, remorse, and shame are examples of emotions people feel when they disregard the moral standards to which they ascribe. Vince, as a former Catholic, is all too familiar with the role of guilt in this religious tradition. But Catholics also formalize the practice of removing guilt through the sacrament of penance, or "confession". Vince remembers the uncomfortable, even scary experience of admitting his "sins" to the parish priest, who sat silently behind an opaque screen in a darkened booth (a recurring offense was swiping a few dimes from the pile of change his dad would leave on his dresser). This ritualized acknowledging of wrongdoing, and subsequent efforts to do "penance" by repeating certain prayers or engaging in good deeds, is intended to wipe the slate clean, while renewing one's relationship with God – a kind of relationship reinvention for sure. Of course, many of us carry unnecessary burdens of guilt, sometimes because we internalized at a young age religious or parental messages which encouraged us to internalize unrealistic standards of behavior.

Vince's experience with guilt can be contrasted with the feeling of shame. Fisher and Exline (2010) identify guilt and remorse as negative emotions associated with a specific action, or wrongdoing ("I feel badly that I told your secret to friends"). In contrast, shame is the negative emotional experience connected to one's perception of oneself ("Letting my friends down is what I always do. I am an unworthy person"). Fisher and Exline (2010) suggest that shame can actually lead to nonproductive responses such as avoidance of one's wrongdoing, aggression to one's partner, or self-destructive responses. For instance, Wietzker, Buysse, Loeys, and Brondeel (2011) found that guilt experienced by divorcing partners was associated with less forcing, and more yielding and problem-solving with one another. Interestingly, shame was associated with classic fight or flight responses, avoidance and aggression, and less problem-solving. Kelley (2017) suggests that shame undermines the emotional foundation needed for behavioral change. That is, if one's sense of self is diminished by shame, then self-protective behaviors, such as avoid or attack, are more likely. Alternatively, when one has a healthy sense of self, there is emotional security to apologize for hurtful behavior and take responsibility to work with one's partner on co-creating a positive future.

Guilt can serve an important function. In attending to their guilt people sometimes realize that their behavior is inconsistent with their values. That recognition may prompt them to address misdeeds or to speak up when others encourage behavior that feels wrong. Giving voice to our felt emotions is one way we express and sometimes question the moral agreements that guide us at home and at work. Of course, other emotions can prompt this rethinking. One that comes to mind is moral outrage, a kind of anger that can motivate us to speak up when we are victims or observers of behavior that feels deeply unjust or wrong (Bies, 1987). If you know that a friend is being mistreated by a romantic partner, this feeling might prompt you to encourage your friend to seek counseling. Similarly, if you are the victim of blatant unfairness at work, your moral emotions might prompt you to defend yourself or seek another job. And if you have committed a wrong, your feeling remorse is an important step toward repairing the harm you have done to others.

"Positive" emotions can also function to change and deepen the moral commitments we feel toward others. Consider pride and admiration. We feel proud of ourselves when we do good things for our partners and ourselves. Expressing pride in your partners, or kids, or work team is a way of reinforcing the values that you share. In doing so you acknowledge the goodness of those you care about or admire. These kinds of communication can deepen our relationships and enhance our self-respect.

Humility is another moral emotion with potentially positive connotations. Humbly acknowledging that certain forces in the world are bigger than us – the awe-inspiring beauty of nature, the goodwill of a community to which you belong, the spiritual connections that you feel to a deity or transcendent power –

leads people to look beyond their own needs (which are, of course, important) to consider the greater good. A recent study of awe-inspired behavior examined the kindness that fellow pedestrians displayed to a person who had spilled their belongings on the sidewalk (Piff, Dietze, Feinberg, Stancato, & Keltner, 2015). Walkers who had been encouraged to feel awe (by gazing at the huge trees lining the walkway) were more likely to help gather the spilled belongings. Why? Apparently, the feeling of awe signaled a sense that all of us people are bonded by our relative insignificance. This in turn encouraged strangers to behave more generously and altruistically. That is, the emotional experience of awe transforms relationships even among strangers. In another example, the year 2017 was marked by a major eclipse of the sun, viewed by millions of people around the world. News reports showed awe-struck observers marvel-ing in wonder and turning to embrace the people around them, even those they barely knew.

Clearly, morality-based emotions have the potential to reshape our relation-ships, sometimes in desirable ways. The upshot? Listen to them. Express them. And, as suggested by the study of pedestrians and the big trees, you might even seek experiences to create them.

The Bonding Function: Drawing Us Close

When Doug and Vince started studying communication, back in the 1980s, it was widely believed that self-disclosure was a key to better personal relationships. Just say what you *really* feel or think, suggested many self-help books of the day, and your relationships will flourish. Well, as it turned out, unedited self-disclosure may not be such a good idea after all. More recent theoretical models, such as Petronio's Privacy Management Theory (2018), portray the release of private information as a strategic activity, one guided by such considerations as the nature of one's communication goals and the kind of relationship one wishes to have with the recipient. For example, unbridled venting of angry feelings may leave those on the receiving end feeling attacked, wary, or puzzled about your motives for sharing too much information (TMI). Similarly, people who continually share negative feelings about the past, without a sense of healthy growth over time, can exhaust the patience and goodwill of even the most caring listener. Unabated negative rumination wears down the attentive friend and may leave the sharer feeling depressed.

Having offered those caveats, it is certainly the case that the responsible expression of emotion is both healthy and necessary if you hope to be closely connected to others. In sharing our fears, we communicate trust in our peers or partners. By listening with care during these moments of vulnerability we earn that trust and show that we care. In this regard, Kelley (2012) frames intimacy as a process of granting access to the most vulnerable feelings, most typically fear (although positive emotions, such as love or hope, may increase our vulnerability as well). When our relational worlds are working the way most of us hope they will, the trust involved in this process facilitates a full sense of love, characterized by a deep emotional bond between partners (Kelley, 2012). Of course, privacy also manifests in the decision to withhold or disguise emotion, which can create distance between partners. We all need private moments to sort out feelings, identify their sources, and think about how the other party might react to the expression of our "true feelings", but even so, communicating our need for privacy can be a means of co-creating meaningful relationship rhythms and spaces with our partners.

Based on our own long experience in family relationships and marriages, it has become obvious that unexpressed emotions can be the source of lingering conflict. Vince and his spouse Kathleen recently discovered that unresolved bitterness over events from the distant past was haunting their relationship. In the early years together, Vince's workaholic tendencies led him to lose track of time when he was deeply engaged in research projects. He sometimes arrived home well after the agreed-upon time, leaving Kathleen to tend to their small child while cutting into her own work time. Understandably, Kathleen found this behavior to be disrespectful and she grew deeply resentful. But for a number of reasons, including her fear that expressed conflict was a sign of weakness in a marriage, Kathleen withheld these feelings. Only in recent years, decades later, was this grievance fully aired. The conversation was uncomfortable, but in the end, it removed a barrier to their intimacy – a barrier that was largely hidden below the surface. In instances like this, we see that the expression of emotion, even if much delayed, can be the catalyst of relationship renewal.

Indeed, emotion is often the driver of relationship change, for better or for worse. And we are often unaware of the emotions that lurk below the surface of relationships, dragging them down or even sinking them altogether. Tapping these deep emotions is often difficult and it may require the guidance and safety provided by a skilled therapist or counselor. In some cases, the unearthing of emotions also surfaces difficult truths, as it did for Kathleen and Vince. But in the responsible sifting of emotion, partners may uncover what feels like a more authentic self, the one that was buried under a self-protective impulse to hide vulnerability or disguise feelings that "shouldn't" exist. Owning emotions is one way of expressing respect for self, and sharing them honestly can signal respect for those we care about. In this way, emotional communication functions to make our relationships closer.

The Repair Function: Helping Us Heal

Certain of our emotions play important roles in the healing of damaged relationships. Later, in *Chapter 6*, we discuss the role of emotion in the process of forgiveness. Indeed, voicing the emotions that follow harmful conduct is one of the key "tasks" in our Communicative Tasks of Forgiveness (CTF) model (Waldron & Kelley, 2008). As with each of the tasks, this one takes collective effort, one that involves all parties in identifying and legitimizing the emotional fallout that accompanies serious relational transgressions. One such emotion is hurt, the pain that one feels in response to the injurious words and actions of others. As Kelley (2012) has noted, the emotion of hurt is commonplace in relational conflict and dysfunction. The capacity to acknowledge the hurt we feel or have caused, to understand its severity, and make sense of its origins are crucial tasks if damaged relationships are to be healed.

Remorse is an emotion people feel when they acknowledge the harm and pain they have caused others. In fact, the feeling of remorse can itself be painful in the sense that we feel disturbed and uncomfortable by the harm we have caused others. Remorse is associated with sorrow and it often motivates people to apologize and try to make things better. In contrast, regret is the wish that you had (or had not) taken a particular action. But regret lacks the emotional "oomph" of remorse and it is often focused on negative consequences for the self. You might regret your actions because they led to negative consequences, damaged a valued relationship, or forced you to "miss out" on an opportunity. But expressions of remorse can be transformative. Those who have been hurt often evaluate apologies by the degree to which they seem remorseful (Said, Harink, & Ellemers, 2017). Remorse is often conveyed nonverbally in the form of tears, a mournful countenance, a shaking voice. If judged to be genuine, these are signs that the transgressor is also feeling pain, that he or she appreciates the magnitude of the transgression. Assured of that, victims may become more open to other acts of atonement, such as offers of compensation and pledges to better behavior in the future. In this way, remorse can be a catalyst to relational healing and the eventual restoration of the violator to a family, friendship circle, or community.

Comforting is another communicative form of emotion that helps those who are experiencing emotional anguish (Burleson, 2008). We do it by being present, assuring, and responsive when others are feeling pain, by legitimizing the emotions of a person who is hurt or grieving, and sometimes, by offering help or advice in a way that is useful to the person who is struggling to solve a problem.

Finally, we would like to highlight a few insights from a somewhat recent approach to couples counseling, *Emotionally Focused Therapy (EFT)*. Conceptually founded in attachment theory, EFT seeks to (re)establish a secure base of emotional attachment between partners through a process of cycle de-esclalation, restructuring attachment, and consolidation (Wiebe & Johnson, 2017). In this way, EFT serves both emotional functions of bonding and repair or, better put, repair through bonding. Attachment insecurity in a relationship decreases one's sense of safety and limits one's ability to demonstrate relationship resilience through emotional balance and positive affect regulation. Essentially, a paucity of attachment security may facilitate communication patterns associated with relationship distress and deterioration, such as negative reciprocity and demand/withdraw

(Caughlin & Vangelisti, 2006). In a review of EFT research, Wiebe and Johnson (2017) conclude that EFT can help couples create a more secure attachment and experience affect co-regulation such that they increase their resiliency.

Doug's take on EFT comes from having a Master of Counseling degree and from going through EFT with his wife. After experiencing a number of traumatic experiences in their midlife marriage, Ann and Doug ended up with an EFT counselor that came highly recommended. In essence, some of the problems they were experiencing were rooted in not feeling emotionally safe with one another. The EFT process helped them, safely, become emotionally vulnerable in each other's presence. As they became more securely attached to one another, they also demonstrated more resilience as they modified key patterns in their relationship, such as better learning to accept one another without judgment, and more effectively showing respect.

Emotional Intelligence: Four Competencies for Relational Reimagination

Since at least the 1980s, relationship researchers have realized that intelligence involves more than high cognitive functioning and academic prowess. Emotional intelligence (EI), a term popularized by psychologist Goleman (1995/2005), involves a set of competencies that appear to facilitate success in school, work, and human relationships. While the concept of EI is wide reaching, and there has been some debate about its essential components, Goleman has described competencies related to self-awareness, self-regulation, motivation, empathy, and social skills. Later analyses have narrowed that set to four (Mayer, Salovey, & Caruso, 2008), each of which is described below.

Perception

One dimension of EI is the ability to recognize emotional cues displayed by other people. This would include such vital activities as recognizing that your partner is agitated or upset, noticing that you have embarrassed someone in public, or recognizing the above-mentioned indicators of remorse. This ability hinges in part on attentiveness to nonverbal cues, such as your partner's tone of voice, the embarrassed person's reddening face, or the remorseful transgressor's facial expressions. Those who recognize these cues are better prepared to adapt their verbal behavior to the emotional tone of the moment by (as examples) asking "Is there something wrong?" or offering "I am sorry if I made you uncomfortable". Subsequent interaction might then confirm if the emotional perception was accurate (nonverbal cues can be ambiguous) and whether emotionally responsive communication would be helpful. For example, a distressed partner may appreciate your comforting or soothing remarks, and a child who is exhibiting signs of fear may need assurances. Recognizing and acknowledging the emotions of others can be an intimate act, one that affirms the closeness of some relationships and potentially strengthens the bonds of relationships that have grown distant or frayed.

Understanding

Emotional understanding refers to the knowledge we have of the causes of our emotions and those of others. In the previous example, Vince came to understand Kathleen's anger as a response to disrespect she felt from him years before. The anger persisted, in part because the pair had never really acknowledged its cause. Indeed, the attributions we make about the causes of emotion can shape our responses to them (Metts, 2018; Weiner, 2006). Vince's view of the past focused on his own workload and stress, an explanation that partly excused his tardiness and made Kathleen's anger seem less "justified". By contrast, Kathleen viewed Vince's behavior as intentional, or at least selfish in its lack of regard for her own goals and needs. Anger seems justified when it is attributed to intentional wrong-doing. The proclivity to understand emotional causes can be transformative in relationships, especially when it prompts a discussion of differing views of the circumstances which gave rise to emotion, as it did (eventually) for Kathleen and Vince.

Empathy, the ability to understand and share the emotions of others, is a crucial element of relationship reimagination processes. For example, psychologists have posited that the ability to empathize with an offender facilitates a victim's efforts to be forgiving (Worthington, 1998). The idea is that, in the minds of victims, perpetrators may be defined solely by their offensive actions. An empathetic response might involve the "rehumanization" of offenders, to more fully understand them as persons, including the life circumstances that led them to offend. Perhaps they have had experiences that led them to feel hurt, bitter, angry, fearful, or alienated and these in turn have led them to take action that hurt others. According to Worthington, empathy may arise from a review of our offenses and our feelings of gratitude to those who forgave us. Although these insights do not excuse "bad" behavior, developing richer understandings of the causes of emotional experience is a creative activity that may help us reimagine relationships defined by disappointment, animosity, or estrangement.

Managing

This ability involves the regulation of emotion (Mayer et al., 2008). At times, emotional management involves restraint. Emotionally intelligent persons seem competent at such tasks as reining in anger, modulating arousal, limiting prideful boasting, curbing enthusiasm, and calming fears. In the realm of relationships, these moves can be beneficial in several ways. One of these involves adaptation to social roles. Generally speaking, societies socialize members to produce certain kinds of emotional performances (Waldron, 2000). At work, service employees are expected to accept the emotional venting of unhappy customers and to limit their own emotional displays to expressions of polite cheerfulness or sympathetic concern. Parents are expected to regulate emotions around their children, and they often hide their most extreme feelings of anger or fear. And most of us have been exposed to the emotional constraints of gender roles. One consequence is that boys and men learn to repress emotions such as fear, or alternatively, to transform prohibited emotions into those that are more acceptable for males, such as anger or contempt.

As suggested above, arousal, the body's energized response to potential threats and interests, pays certain survival dividends. But high levels of arousal can be problematic in relationships, resulting in limitations in cognitive processing and potential behavioral responses. The emotional flooding (Gottman, 1994) often associated with high arousal can lead to runaway conflict, a condition character-ized by partners feeling like the interaction is out of control, in spite of initial positive intentions (Kelley, 2012). This process often results in defensiveness and aggression when a more measured response would be preferable. Emotionally intelligent people are aware of this possibility and they take steps to moderate arousal. Often effective means of arousal reduction are taking a mutually agreed-upon break and changing the environment ("Let's get something to drink and go sit on the patio to finish this discussion"), doing something physical to release arousal (e.g., go for a walk or workout), practicing soothing exercises (e.g., breathing, prayer, or yoga), or communicating with a third party (e.g., safe friend, counselor, or journaling) (Driver, Tabares, Shapiro, Nahm, & Gottman, 2003; Kelley, 2012). It is important to remember that the key to these various strategies is to reduce one's arousal levels to a moderate range and avoid rumination. Once arousal levels are manageable, couples can reality-check their emotions, edit their messages to remove content that sounds combative, and engage more creative responses.

Of course, emotional regulation also involves the willful production of positive emotion. If you have ever been told to "cheer up" because your dark feelings were dampening the emotions of your companions, you are familiar with this idea. In fact, emotionally intelligent people may be those who can find ways to produce positive affect where it might not otherwise exist. This can be accom-plished in a number of ways – by reminding yourself of more positive times, by exposing yourself to humorous people or media, by offering yourself compliments or affirmations. And of course, we can create these positive experiences for others using similar devices. In fact, research has long suggested that couples who create more positive emotional experiences are more likely to stay together (Gottman, 1999). The theory of social capital suggests that such behaviors as giving compliments, creating fun experiences, and making positive plans for the future create a bank of positivity that can be "drawn down" when the relationship is threatened by hardship (Feeney & LeMay, 2012).

Harnessing

Emotion can be used for motivational purposes, to push people to advance toward their relational goals. And it is often used for that purpose in organizations (Waldron, 2012). This harnessing dimension of EI is often enacted strategically, through emotional communication. For example, fear appeals are often used to meet persuasive goals. Parents may issue grave warnings to their children, so they fear the consequences of drug abuse, unsafe driving, or unprotected sex. In fact, the elicitation of emotions in others is an important relational skill, enacted by such behaviors as offering humorous anecdotes to stimulate mirth, sharing woes to elicit sympathy, wielding criticism to cultivate humility, and numerous other goal-directed actions. If partners desire to make relationships closer, more authentic, more supportive, more fun – emotional communication helps them do so.

And yet, forms of emotional communication can also be deployed as relational weaponry. Waldron (2009b) has written about the ways in which emotional tyrants harm others, often by manipulating their emotions. Among the tools of emotional tyrants are mockery, sarcasm, shaming, guilting, intimidating, and the grinding down of emotional defenses. Emotional intelligence is no guarantee of ethical behavior and it is entirely possible that those who are most emotionally intelligent are best prepared to be manipulative as well as emotionally supportive (see Dougherty & Krone, 2002). In this sense, emotions can be harnessed to transform relationships for better or for worse. So, in considering how to reimagine relationships, partners might first examine the goals of the emotional communication they share, culling out the destructive ones and pursuing the constructive ones more mindfully.

A Few Emotional Issues

Before wrapping up this chapter, we want to raise a few emotional issues. The word *emotional* is a good place to start. It is too often used simplistically and with a negative connotation. One meaning of emotional is "out of control", as in public weeping or unhinged displays of anger. We hope it is clear at this point that emotional expressions can be uncontrolled or controlled, strategic or spontaneous, manipulative or authentic.

It has also been common for social scientists to discuss emotions as either positive or negative (Guerrero & LaValley, 2006). Classically, emotions such as sadness and anger are viewed as negative, and happiness and contentment as positive. Yet, this simple bifurcation is insufficient, at best, to help us negotiate the complex emotional landscape. To this point, Fitness and Williams (2013) suggest that anger, while typically assigned negative valence, may indeed feel energizing and satisfying, and joy's typical pleasurability can be alarming when it shades toward mania. Likewise, sadness over the loss of a good friend, while agonizing at one level, may be deeply beautiful at another.

Finally, understanding emotional responses in relationships is complicated by the fact that experience or expression of certain emotions can mask that of others. Anger is commonly called a secondary emotion because fear often underlies angry responses – think of the fear-based anger you experience when your favorite pooch dashes across the road in front of traffic, or how anger directed toward one of your children might actually be masking fear of losing respect. Sanford's (2007, 2012) discussion of soft (sadness and hurt) and hard (angry, annoyed) emotions provides further insight into the nature of emotion-masking. Soft emotions are characterized by attachment and closeness, and this resulting vulnerability can be met with protective responses associated with the power and self-preservation of harder emotions such as anger. In other words, anger at a close friend who is unexpectedly moving may be masking the deep pain of being "abandoned". If partners fail to recognize these emotional nuances, they risk misunderstanding, for instance, reading their partner's anger as a sign of disinterest in the relationship.

Emotional Conclusions

This chapter underscores how the emotions people experience, and the ways in which they are communicated, color our relationships in shades both dark and bright. As we conclude, several integrating themes come to mind. First, we know that despite their powerful pull on us, emotions often operate without our full awareness. Our feelings are subverted by our roles, the forces of socialization, or the manipulative efforts of others. Though we may choose not to acknowledge them, emotions remain potent sources of satisfaction and disgruntlement in our encounters with others. (Re)discovering our emotions is a worthwhile activity.

Second, emotional communication is a powerful shaper of human relationships. Our efforts to more fully understand the emotions of others may pay off in a deeper kind of knowing, improved possibilities for navigating conflicts, and a greater likelihood of healing relational hurt. Third, we have seen that emotional communication can harm as well as help. Developing emotional intelligence is a laudable goal, one that might be achieved by taking relationship classes, seeking feedback from emotionally intelligent friends, or meeting with a trusted counselor. This kind of personal investment may result in improved relational outcomes. And yet, we should be aware that we can be both victim and perpetrator of emotional manipulation. Finally, we note that emotions might be thought of as a wellspring of emotional creativity. Deeply felt emotions, even those which are unwelcome, are often a catalyst for change, and the reimagination of oneself and one's relationships.

References

Aristotle. (2000). *Nicomachean ethics, book VIII* (R. Crisp, Trans.). Cambridge, UK: Cambridge University Press.

Bembenek, A. F., Beilke, D. R., & Schroeder, D. A. (2007). Justice violations, emotional, reactions, and justice-seeking responses. In D. de Cremer (Ed.), *Advances in the psychology of justice and affect* (pp. 15–36). Charlotte, NC: Information Age Publishing.

Bies, R. J. (1987). The predicament of injustice: The management of moral outrage. In L. L. Cummings & B. M. Staw (Eds.), *Research in organizational behavior* (Vol. 9, pp. 289–319). Greenwich, CT: JAI Publishers.

Burleson, B. R. (2008). What counts as effective emotional support: Explorations of individual and situational differences. In M. Motley (Ed.), *Studies in applied interpersonal communication* (pp. 207–228). Los Angeles, CA: Sage.

Caughlin, J. P., & Vangelisti, A. L. (2006). Conflict in dating and marital relationships. In J. G. Oetzel & S. Ting-Toomey (Eds.), *SAGE handbook of conflict communication: Integrating theory, research, and practice* (pp. 129–157). Thousand Oaks, CA: Sage.

Darwin, C. (1871). *The descent of man.* London, UK: John Murray.

Darwin, C. (1998). *The expression of the emotions in man and animals* (3rd ed.). New York, NY: Oxford University Press. (Original work published 1872)

de Becker, G. (1997) *The gift of fear and other survival signals that protect us from violence.* New York, NY: Dell Publishing.

de Cremer, D. (2007). *Advances in the psychology of justice and affect.* Charlotte, NC: Information Age Publishing.

Dougherty, D., & Krone, K. J. (2002). Emotional intelligence as organizational communication: An examination of the construct. In W. B. Gudykunst (Ed.), *Communication yearbook 26* (pp. 202–229). Newbury Park, CA: Sage.

Driver, J., Tabares, A., Shapiro, A., Nahm, E. Y., & Gottman, J. M. (2003). Interactional patterns in marital success and failure: Gottman laboratory studies. In F. Walsh (Ed.), *Normal family processes: Growing diversity and complexity* (3rd ed., pp. 493–513). New York, NY: Guilford Press.

English, T., Oliver P. J., & Gross, J. J. (2013). Emotion regulation in close relationships. In J. Simpson & L. Campbell (Eds.), *The Oxford handbook of close relationships.* doi:10.1093/oxfordhb/9780195398694.013.0022

Feeney, B. C., & Lemay, E. P. (2012). Surviving relationship threats: The role of emotional capital. *Personality and Social Psychology Bulletin, 38,* 1004–1017.

Feldman Barrett, L., Lewis, M., & Haviland-Jones. J. M. (2018). *Handbook of emotions* (4th ed.). New York, NY: Guilford Press.

Fisher, M. L., & Exline, J. J. (2010). *Moving toward self-forgiveness: Removing barriers related to shame, guilt, and regret.* Oxford, UK. doi:10.1111/j.1751–9004.2010.00276.x

Fitness, J., & Williams, V. (2013). The features and functions of positive emotions in close relationships. In M. Hojjat & D. Cramer, D. (Eds.), *Positive psychology of love* (pp. 44–56). New York, NY: Oxford University Press.

Floyd, K., Dinsmore, D. R., & Pavlich, C. A. (2018). The theory of natural selection: An evolutionary approach to family communication. In D. O. Braithwaite, E. A. Suter, & K. Floyd (Eds.), *Engaging theories in family communication: Multiple perspectives* (pp. 312–323). New York, NY: Routledge.

Goleman, D. (2005). *Emotional intelligence. Why it can matter more than IQ.* New York, NY: Bantam Books. (Original work published 1995.)

Gottman, J. M. (1994). *What predicts divorce?* Hillsdale, NJ: Lawrence Erlbaum.

Gottman, J. M. (1999). *The marriage clinic: A scientifically based marital therapy*. New York, NY: W.W. Norton.

Guerrero, L. K., & Cole, M. (2015). Moral standards, emotions, and communication associated with relationship transgressions in dating relationships. In V. Waldron & D. Kelley (Eds.), *Moral talk across the lifespan: Creating good relationships* (pp. 155–181). New York, NY: Peter Lang.

Guerrero, L. K, & LaValley, A. G. (2006). Conflict, emotion, and communication. In J. G. Oetzel & S. Ting-Toomey (Eds.), *The SAGE handbook of conflict communication: Integrating theory, research, and practice* (pp. 69–96). Thousand Oaks, CA: Sage.

Haidt, J. (2003). The moral emotions. In R. J. Davidson, K. R. Scherer, & H. H. Goldsmith (Eds.), *Handbook of affective sciences* (pp. 852–870). Oxford, UK: Oxford University Press.

Kelley, D. L. (2012). *Marital communication*. Cambridge, UK: Polity Press.

Kelley, D. L. (2017). *Just relationships: Living out social justice as mentor, family, friend, and lover.* New York, NY: Routledge.

Keltner, D. (2009). *Born to be good: The science of a meaningful life*. New York, NY: W.W. Norton.

Mayer, J. D., Salovey, P., & Caruso, D. R. (2008). Emotional intelligence: New ability or eclectic traits? *American Psychologist, 63*, 503–517.

Metts, S. (2018). Appraisal theories of emotion. In D. Braithwaite, E. Suter, & K. Floyd (Eds.), *Engaging theories of family communication* (2nd ed., pp. 27–37). New York, NY: Taylor & Francis.

Nussbaum, M. C. (2016). *Anger and forgiveness: Resentment, generosity, justice*. New York, NY: Oxford University Press.

Petronio, S. (2018). Communication privacy management theory: Understanding families. In D. O. Braithwaite, E. A. Suter, & K. Floyd (Eds.), *Engaging theories in family communication* (2nd ed., pp. 87–97). New York, NY: Taylor & Francis.

Piff, P. K., Dietze, P., Feinberg, M., Stancato, D. M., & Keltner, D. (2015). Awe, the small self, and prosocial behavior. *Journal of Personality and Social Psychology, 108*(6), 883–899. doi:10.1037/pspi0000018

Said, S., Harink, F., & Ellemers, N. (2017) Sorry seems to be the hardest word: Cultural differences in apologizing effectively. *Journal of Applied Social Psychology, 47*, 553–557. doi:10.1111/jasp.12460

Sanford, K. (2007). The couples emotion rating form: Psychometric properties and theoretical associations. *Journal of Social and Personal Relationships, 20*, 391–402.

Sanford, K. (2012). The communication of emotion during conflict in married couples. *Journal of Family Psychology, 26*(3), 297–307. doi:10.1037/a0028139

TED. (2012, March 16). *Brené Brown: Listening to shame* [Video file]. Retrieved from https://ted.com/talks/brene_brown_listening_to_shame

Waldron, V. R. (2000). Relational experiences and emotion at work. In S. Fineman (Ed.), *Emotion in organizations* (2nd ed., pp. 64–82). Thousand Oaks, CA: Sage.

Waldron, V. R. (2009a). Emotional tyranny at work: Suppressing the moral emotions. In P. Lutgen-Sandvick & B. Davenport-Sypher (Eds.), *Destructive organizational practices: Processes, consequences, and constructive ways of organizing* (pp. 9–26). New York, NY: Routledge.

Waldron, V. R. (2009b). Emotional tyranny and managerial power. In P. Lutgen-Sandvik & B. Davenport-Sypher (Eds.), *The destructive side of organizational communication* (pp. 7–26). New York, NY: Routledge.

Waldron, V. R. (2012). *Communicating emotion at work*. Malden, MA: Polity Press.

Waldron, V. R., & Kelley, D. L. (2008). *Communicating forgiveness*. Thousand Oaks, CA: Sage.

Weiner, B. (2006). *Social motivation, justice, and the moral emotions: An attributional approach*. Mahwah, NJ: Lawrence Erlbaum.

Wietzker, A., Buysse, A., Loeys, T., & Brondeel, R. (2011). Easing the conscience: Feeling guilty makes people cooperate in divorce negotiations. *Journal of Social and Personal Relationships, 29*, 324–336.

Wiebe, S. A., & Johnson, S. M. (2017). Creating relationships that foster resilience in emotionally focused therapy. *Current Opinion in Psychology, 13*, 65–69. doi:10.1016/j.copsyc.2016.05.001

Worthington, E. L. (1998). *Dimensions of forgiveness: Psychological research and theological perspectives*. Philadelphia, PA: Templeton Foundation Press.

5

SENSE-MAKING

Understanding Relational Change

Shana worked as an assistant youth minister in a large church, but her relationship with the youth minister (Y.M.) was complicated because the pair had dated briefly in the past. Y.M. had "trouble letting go" of his feelings for Shana. Over time she grew weary and resentful of his "inappropriate comments". These frustrations were a contributing factor in her decision to leave the job. Shana explains what happened about one month later:

> *Y.M. set a date to have lunch with me and we talked. At this time he apologized and explained that he felt responsible for my leaving. Because I hadn't given it much thought at the time, I told him, 'No problem. No, you weren't the cause.' But after doing some soul searching and trying to address the roots of some of my anger, I realize he did owe me an apology. At the time of the lunch I forgave him but not with much thought. For him this settled it. He felt better knowing that I forgave him. But now I feel like I need to forgive him again. Because I hadn't really come to terms for why I was forgiving him then. I still have doubts about him – and our relationship has not grown or gotten stronger.*

★

We are thrust into reimagining our relationships when calamity strikes, when developmental change pushes us to find better ways of responding to new contingencies, and, as in Shana's case, when our "real feelings" are out of synch with our external behaviors. Whatever motivates our move toward change, we inevitably engage in a process of sense-making to contend with life's surprises, our sense that something is wrong, even if we can't quite put our finger on the problem. At times, making sense of our uncertainty is intentional ("Let's sit down and discuss what happened and what it means for our future"), while other sense-making responses such as rumination (e.g., "Why is this happening to me? I can't believe this is happening, again. What's wrong with me?") and tangential coherence (e.g., "What should I do? I trusted you! I'm going to bed, you can sleep in the guest room") are marked by a sense of feeling out of control, heightened arousal and emotion, and being victimized by our own runaway thinking (Kelley, 2012).

Shana's story demonstrates the complex process of sense-making. By offering a quick, unprocessed forgiveness, Shana relieved her boss of uncertainty. For him, the matter was "settled". But Shana's uncertainty was prolonged, and possibly even increased. This episode demonstrates how sense-making often involves exploring, managing, and integrating one's emotions and thoughts, over time – often through numerous sense-making attempts to try and get it "right". Once having sifted through the reasons for her anger, Shana concludes that she needs to "forgive him again", but still has "doubts about him" and is uncertain as to their relational future. Clearly Shana will continue to make sense of this relationship for some time to come.

Shana's story highlights the cognitive reorientation that typically accompanies relational disruption, and subsequent relationship transition. Herein we explore the nature of sense-making when partners think that something "wrong" has occurred. The following discussion emphasizes communicative efforts to understand, perspective-take, reduce uncertainty, and, essentially, "make meaning of" what has happened, what is happening, and what possibly can happen to ourselves, our partners, and our relationships.

Sense-Making

Disruptive events become transitional episodes in our lives (see *Chapter 3*), be they relational transgressions ("I trusted you not to tell") or responses to developmental (Brittney, just turned 16, now, has her driver's license!) or environment change (the economy just dipped and now "We are upside down on our mortgage!"). These disruptive episodes create uncertainty, call moral values into question, and force us to reconsider our relational assumptions, reorienting us from the topic or issue at hand to various elements in our relational frame. Relational frames provide the lenses by which we make sense of our relational partners and our connections to them (Kelley, 2017). They are our relational worldviews. Relational Framing Theory (Solomon & McLaren, 2008) proposes two such frames, those of dominance-submissiveness and affiliation-disaffiliation. In essence, it is suggested we interpret relational behavior in terms of control and connection. We may wonder – Who is making the decisions? Does she see me as an equal? Is this behavior drawing us closer?

According to Kelley (2017), relational frames are comprehensive perspectives that include relational themes, such as the aforementioned dominance-submissiveness and affiliation–disaffiliation, but are also influenced by such elements as how we form relational attributions and attachments. For example, Feeney (2005), operating from an attachment perspective, suggests that relational hurt reorients us to consider whether we are loveable, and whether our partners are available, responsive, and trustworthy. In this way relational disruption reorients partners from a focus on instrumental tasks (e.g., getting the oil changed, picking up chicken for dinner) to a focus on their own personal value, their partner's character and potential responsiveness, and the potential future of the relationship. Processes that help partners understand these three elements (self, partner, relationship) include managing relational turbulence, reducing uncertainty, negotiating relational dialectics, blaming and making relational attributions, experiencing and demonstrating empathy and understanding, and determining how to move on (forgive, reconcile, and/or terminate the relationship).

Making Sense Through Relational Turbulence

Relational Turbulence Theory focuses on communication processes that occur during relationship change, in particular, how partners respond to uncertainty and assess their interdependence. Turbulence may result in "polarizing effects on people's cognitive appraisals, emotional reactions, and communication behaviors" (Knobloch, Solomon, Theiss, & McLaren, 2018, p. 257), a consequence of high uncertainty, knowledge deficit, and subsequent biased appraisals of communication events. The effects of these relational assessments are influenced by partners' degree of dependence, and perception as to whether the interruption is blocking a goal or accomplishing a goal. All of this plays out to influence the selection of one's communication strategies, such as whether to express collaboration and supportiveness.

Commonly, relational interruption leads to strong emotional reaction and increased sensitivity to future interruptions. Cumulative effects of repeated turbulence may include a fixation on the proximal confines of a given interaction, reducing the ability to contextualize the event in terms of long-term relational goals (Knobloch et al., 2018). Or, to use a common colloquialism, partners may fail "to see the forest for the trees", getting so caught up in the immediate situation that they lose sight of long-term goals. A few years ago, Dayna was with a friend, Roberta, whose husband had deeply wounded her by having lunch with his ex-wife. Roberta would not have been upset except that she only found out about the luncheon by inadvertently seeing a "thank you" text from the ex-wife on her husband's phone. In the midst of her initial hurt and betrayal, she was bent on embarrassing him at an upcoming family event. However, after venting with Dayna, she began to settle emotionally and was able to see the potential damage this reaction could cause, especially to their children and extended family.

Clearly, such a proximal focus has the potential to limit partners' communicative choices and constrict their abilities to reimagine their relational future. Equally important in this story is recognition that third-party communication is a frequent means of engaging in relational sense-making.

Making Sense of Uncertainty

Uncertainty within the context of one's relationships is magnified by relationship turbulence. Consider the following quote from film classic *Ordinary People* (Schwary & Redford, 1980), where Beth and Calvin discuss their rather turbulent family in the aftermath of their oldest son's (Buck) death:

> Maybe it wasn't even Buck; maybe it was just you. Maybe, finally, it was the best of you that you buried. But, whatever it was . . . I don't know who you are. And I don't know what we've been playing at. So I was crying. Because I don't know if I love you anymore. And I don't know what I'm going to do without that.
>
> – Calvin

The phrase "I don't know" is used four times in this short passage. Calvin's dilemma highlights the dilemma we all experience, namely, how we respond to uncertainty is significant to our ability to reimagine our relational futures.

The study of uncertainty is not new to the social sciences, having emerged in the 1970s (Berger & Calabrese, 1975). Early work hypothesized that individuals are motivated to reduce relational uncertainty. Partners hoping to reduce uncertainty in their relationships were found to use such tactics as questioning, self-disclosures, and consultations with third parties (Berger & Kellermann, 1994).

The Theory of Motivated Information Management (Afifi & Weiner, 2004) is an uncertainty-based theory that provides insight regarding relationship reimagination. This theoretical perspective assumes that information management, and consequently uncertainty reduction, proceeds through stages of *interpretation, evaluation,* and *decision.* Interpretation begins when partners experience a discrepancy between desired and experienced levels of uncertainty. This discrepancy reorients partners to interpret the meaning of the behavior, often triggering anxiety. Elevated levels of uncertainty can also be perceived positively (e.g., Brashers, 2001), bringing stimulation, anticipation, and novelty to a wellworn relationship. Distressed couples might find comfort and hope in uncertainty, in contrast to feeling as though the relationship is in a downward slide.

The second stage generates evaluation of the potential short- and long-term outcomes of seeking information. What are the *likely risks, costs, and benefits*? For example, what are potential consequences of monitoring someone's Facebook page to see who their friends are, as compared to asking third parties? Communicators also evaluate their own potential *efficacy* in modulating levels of uncertainty. Do they know the parlance of 16-year-old culture to find out what's really happening at school? Coping with potentially negative information and assessing the likelihood that a source can provide the needed information are other factors often considered. Consider Matt's complicated situation as an example of efficacy and coping, and weighing the cost of attempting to reduce uncertainty. Matt has always loved to read, and so began a book club with four other male friends. Three years into the book club, Matt noticed one member, Jim, didn't invite him to events outside the book club, although other members were often invited. Matt thought about asking Kevin if Jim had said anything to him, but that felt awkward and vulnerable to Matt, and he wasn't sure if Kevin would be attentive to that kind of thing ("Gee, Matt, to be honest I didn't really notice you haven't been invited"). In addition, Matt was afraid that if he found out Jim was being intentional in excluding him, he would retaliate by kicking Jim out of the book club. Matt ended up saying nothing, just hoping that things would get better.

Ultimately, the final stage involves decision making regarding the selection of information management strategies which are responsive to interpretation and evaluation factors. *Seeking relevant information* is one of three information management strategies (Afifi & Weiner, 2004) and includes such elements as talking directly about the issue, talking indirectly around the issue, and observation. *Avoiding relevant information*, a second strategy, uses active and passive forms of avoidance, such as changing the topic and diversion (e.g., humor) that may allow for optimal timing and moderate arousal levels such that partners are better able to eventually seek, and interpret, relevant information. A third strategy, *cognitive reappraisal*, often involves adjusting the perceived importance or meaning of an action. Our own forgiveness research has provided numerous examples of this approach as partners reframed their now uncertain future as a "new journey", a "test of faith", and "throwing out the rule book and starting over" (Waldron & Kelley, 2008).

Walid Afifi (2012), in a Tedx talk profiling his research on uncertainty, describes the common finding of his numerous uncertainty-based studies as follows: We can successfully manage and negotiate uncertainty in our lives if we know that the person we care about the most, cares about us. In fact, Afifi suggests that relational partners use the phrase, "I am here for you" as a means of helping one another manage the uncertainty in their lives. Afifi's prompt is a powerful encouragement for us all, and also highlights inherent dilemmas in close relationships. For example, consider the struggle this creates for individuals when the source of their uncertainty is their partner. In light of Feeney's (2005) proposal that relational hurt reorients us to assess whether our partner is available, responsive, and trustworthy, it is evident that basing our uncertainty management on those we are closest to, also puts us at significant risk. In the story Doug tells at the end of *Chapter 1*, he recounts how Ann and he were in therapy for over a year. This was a difficult period, in part because they had a number of family deaths during this time, but couldn't really be there for one another emotionally. In couples counseling each partner is working through issues . . . with the very person they would typically go to for support. This highlights the nature of close relationships – our most meaningful conflicts are with the person that means the most to us. When one's significant other is unavailable, having a rich and varied social support network that can provide many of the functions of uncertainty reduction (e.g., giving information, providing perspective, serving as identity anchors) is all the more important.

Managing uncertainty is further complicated because the process may not unfold in a linear way. For instance, an initial arousal-based emotional response triggers sense-making, and subsequent sense-making triggers additional emotional responses, and so forth. What is certain is the reciprocal effect between sense-making and emotional experience. Consider the following example, adapted from Doug's interview with Ricardo and Sabrina:

> *Ricardo and Sabrina pastored a small church in Southern Arizona and were at dinner with the children's ministry director, Rose, and her husband. Ricardo asked a question of Rose and before she could respond, Sabrina offered her opinion. According to Sabrina, at this point, Ricardo glanced at her and said, "Shut up", and then turned back to Rose for her answer. Sabrina wasn't about to let anyone, especially her husband, speak to her this way and she abruptly stood up from the table and left the restaurant. Ricardo was stunned, looked at his friends and then left the restaurant to look for Sabrina, whom he found walking down the country highway toward their home. After some coaxing Sabrina got into the car and when they arrived home they discussed what happened. Ricardo remained unconvinced that he had said "shut up", while Sabrina could still hear the words ringing in her ears. After some time, Ricardo came to the following conclusion, "I didn't think I had done anything wrong. What I thought I had said wasn't improper. But I realized that the dynamics were something far beyond what I was thinking happened. Me being right was less important than Sabrina being hurt. At that point I made a decision to set aside the importance of me being right, and not having done anything wrong, for the sake of caring for her. Exactly what happened we'll never resolve. And that just isn't as important as removing the pain as much as I can."*

Sabrina, surprised at Ricardo's directive to "shut up", was quickly reoriented from thinking about the children's ministry to thinking about her husband, herself, and the nature of her marriage. Her heightened arousal created a strong emotional reaction ("No one speaks to me that way, especially my husband!"), and she exited the situation. Ricardo, equally surprised by Sabrina's accusation, immediately thought how unfair this all seemed ("I didn't think I had done anything wrong"). Significantly, Ricardo kept his negative emotional response from escalating and, instead, reoriented himself to Sabrina's pain, and imagined the relational implications of this having happened.

As Sabrina and Ricardo's story illustrates, severe transgressions heighten relational uncertainty. This reorients the offended party to question the partner's motives and reassess the degree of concordance in partner expectations (Kelley & Waldron, 2005). Elevated uncertainty regarding the partner and relationship future may lead to increased monitoring of partner verbal and nonverbal response. For instance, apology may be gauged carefully for sincerity; explanation for fidelity; a simple statement for veracity. Questioning may become more common ("Why are you 15 minutes late?"). Conditional forgiveness (e.g., "I will forgive you, if . . .") may be used in an effort to safeguard oneself from future harm, attempting to reduce uncertainty through stability and promise.

The Theory of Motivated Information Management (Afifi & Weiner, 2004) also suggests that individuals will be more interested in seeking out information with large discrepancies. While it is somewhat intuitive that more sense-making communication would follow serious transgressions, certain conditions may alter this effect. For instance, if the offended partner believes that the transgression is an unforgivable offense (e.g., infidelity or intentional hurtful behavior) under *any* circumstance, the offended party may be less motivated to reduce uncertainty ("I don't want to know. I'm done with this relationship!"). One may also deem that information seeking is too costly. It may not seem worth the effort to attend counseling or probe friends for new insights. Alternatively, when partners view relational turmoil and hurt as forgivable or, even, acceptable (e.g., developmental struggles with a teenage son), they may choose communication that *sustains* uncertainty about the future of the relationship, in the hope that continued interaction will reveal possible paths to reconciliation.

When Ann and Doug were trying to maintain the family while their youngest son was dropping out of high school, they intentionally tolerated a high degree of ambiguity and uncertainty (although they also set appropriate boundaries) in the hopes that Daniel would eventually desire to recommit to the family. In the short run, their commitment to Daniel and their hopes for a new version of "us" as family led to increased uncertainty and stress as they reimagined their long-range goals. This process fits with *Relational Turbulence Theory* predictions, discussed previously, that turmoil can result in proximal, as opposed to long-range, thinking. In Ann and Doug's case they avoided being "suffocated" by the present situation (proximal), through strong support from their social network and a determination to stay focused on creating a safe space for Daniel to return (Kelley, 2017).

Making Sense Through Negotiating Relational Dialectics

Another approach partners use to make sense of relationship struggles is the negotiation of relational dialectics. From a dialectical perspective, relationships are always in flux. Partners use communication to manage a series of "contradictory motivations" that *inevitably* arise when the needs and values of two or more individuals are merged in a relationship. For example, most romantic partners express a motivation to be emotionally close to their partners, yet are also at times motivated to create emotional distance when they feel vulnerable or emotionally exhausted. Similarly, when relational stress enters the picture, partners use dialogue and nonverbal positioning to adjust to the changing environment – for instance, becoming more united and interdependent in response to a crisis, but then reasserting individual autonomy as the situation normalizes.

Central themes of the dialectical framework are contradiction and dialogue (Baxter, 2003). *Contradiction* emerges when relational partners' unique identities result in relational tensions, such as closedness/openness, interdependence/ autonomy, or novelty/predictability. The relationship stays in flux, as partners verbally and nonverbally, explicitly and implicitly, negotiate these elements (Baxter & Montgomery, 1996), establishing meaning in the relationship in the process (Baxter, 2011). This is a potentially useful construct for partners who are struggling – flux, micro and macro changes are normal relationship processes essential to making our relationships meaningful.

Unity of opposites is another dialectical construct of theoretical and practical use. Here the idea of unity is not used to emphasize the importance of similarity in relationships (although clearly similarity plays an important role), but rather unity represents the struggle and beauty of integrating opposing forces. You need down time; I need to talk. Our ability to collaboratively integrate these opposing forces creates a significant form of unity and provides a significant perspective for imaginatively managing partner differences.

Baxter and colleagues (Baxter & Montgomery, 1996; Baxter & West, 2003) discuss multiple communicative methods of managing dialectical tensions, several of which are pertinent to the process of reimagining our relationships. One approach is to separate or *sequence* opposing concepts. Essentially, to minimize the relational tension, each polar opposite is expressed at different points in time or in different contexts. For example, romantic partners in the early stages of counseling may manage the dialectic of openness/closedness by talking openly during counseling sessions, and restricting communication between sessions.

Another approach is to actively *embrace* one side of the relational tension while downplaying the other. This is often the case with autonomy/connection when one partner is diagnosed with an illness, such as cancer. For example, when Ted was diagnosed with lymphoma, he and his wife, Jen, literally embraced connection (more hugs, more time together) as they sought to negotiate the uncertainty that lay before them. *Integration* of opposites is a third strategy wherein both poles of the dialectic are expressed simultaneously. In the previous example regarding Ted's cancer, Ted and Jen also chose to manage uncertainty by integrating predictability and novelty into a new family ritual of regularly having dinner together (predictability) and making certain that those dinners included conversations about new discoveries and information regarding procedures, tests, and chemo (novelty).

Finally, a common approach to managing apparent contradictions is to *reframe* the dialectical tension. For example, romantic couples may experience tension when one partner is making a new career move. Is it "my" choice or "our" decision? Rather than viewing this as a struggle between autonomy and interdependence, the couple can reframe this as an "adventure", a chance for personal and relational growth. This kind of reframing moves a potentially difficult discussion toward collaborative imagination of a positive future.

Waldron and Kelley (2008) and Kloeber (2011) have identified specific dialectical tensions that emerge when relationships are difficult and in transition, specifically, when negotiating relationship transgressions. Kloeber (2011) discovered reconcilable/irreconcilable to be the most prevalent tension among conditional forgivers. This dialectic represents the imaginative struggle present with most partners dealing with severe relationship struggles – "Can I imagine myself ever *not* feeling this pain?", "I can't ever picture myself trusting her again".

Mercy–justice was the most salient dialectic in Waldron and Kelley's (2008) work. This classic tension when things go "wrong" is enacted through expressions of compassion, generosity, empathy, acceptance *and/or* resentment, unilateral moves, and revenge. Revenge is a communication act often designed to get justice or "even the score" (Kelley, 2017; Yoshimura & Boon, 2018). In fact, when proportionate to the offense, revenge can even be appreciated as poetic justice (Baxter, Pederson, & Norwood, 2015). Revenge takes various forms. It can be overt or covert, characterized by approach or avoidance (Yoshimura & Boon, 2018). For example, one woman reported she dated her ex-boyfriend's friend just "to get back at him", whereas another used the "silent treatment" as a form of punishment. In contrast, some couples actively suppress their desire for revenge and engage *mercifully* with their partner. As a husband in one of our studies recommended regarding mercy over revenge, "It's not worth fighting when you have been together this long. You just end up hurting each other and not solving the problem."

Another dialectical struggle that emerged during relational tribulation is *remembering–forgetting* (Waldron & Kelley, 2008). Participants in our studies of forgiveness frequently verbalized the tension between remembering and forgetting relational transgressions. Remembering unpleasant experiences is often deemed necessary if mistakes of the past are to be avoided in the present, and commonly therapists recommend recall of positive shared experiences as a means of reinforcing a couple's bond and generating positive emotions that may eventually replace negative (Worthington, 2006). At the same time, partners may wish to forget or suppress negative experiences and the emotions that accompany them in order to remain focused on the relational present, or may "practically forget" by choosing not to bring up past incidents in present conversations.

Heart–mind represents another important relational dialectic (Kloeber, 2011; Waldron & Kelley, 2008). As we explored in the preceding chapter, relational trauma spurs intense emotional response along with coinciding cognitive assessment and speculation. The pull between "heart" and "head" can be seen in the credence many people give to a heartfelt apology over a carefully articulated explanation. In contrast, thoughtful choices can have significant relational consequences. For instance, after her husband's affair, Sally made an intellectual *decision* to forgive before she *felt* like forgiving.

> Therapists say you don't have to forgive in the beginning; you have to work at it. Well, I learned you could forgive in the beginning. Even if you just mouth it in your heart. Because there is something to saying, "I forgive you . . ." And then you start building on that . . .
>
> (Waldron & Kelley, 2008, p. 63)

A final dialectic identified by Waldron and Kelley (2008) is *trust–risk*. Clearly, relational change that results from interpersonal transgressions degrades trust, but uncertainty stemming from developmental or environmental change can also undermine trust. The reimagination of our relationships is a process of rebuilding trust, while reducing the risk of future damage to self or partner behavior or environmental contingencies. Listen to Karla's words as she struggles with wanting "a real marriage", after her husband's affair, while simultaneously being afraid to trust, again:

> *I'm still working through the forgiveness . . . and I think I'm getting there. I know we're going to stay married. There's no question in my mind and I know we're going to have a good marriage. And I don't know if there'll be 100% trust ever again. I don't know. Right now, I don't feel trust. But, I think you can forgive and still have to . . . hopefully we can get to that point again. You know, I'm afraid to be vulnerable, but at the same time, I don't want a marriage where we're just going through the motions so that we stayed married. I want a marriage, I mean a real marriage.*
>
> (Waldron & Kelley, 2008, p. 65)

Karla's struggle is really the struggle of all relational partners who seek to reimagine their relationships. Reimagination always places us in tension between risk and trust. To relationally move toward what one can imagine, but doesn't yet exist, inevitably puts us at risk. Yet, the very act of moving toward a jointly reimagined future can be trust's rebirth.

Kloeber (2011) found a related, but slightly distinct tension from trust–risk, in her analysis of conditional forgivers: Safety-risk (i.e., how emotionally and/or physically safe does this relationship feel?) This fine distinction might be a reflection of the serious nature of transgressions that are often associated with conditional forgiveness (Merolla & Zhang, 2011; Waldron & Kelley, 2005). In such cases, reimagining relationships might mean creating some healthy distance. For example, one of Kloeber's participants shared that while drinking heavily, "My husband called me bad things and said he was going to slash my face with a knife" (p. 16). Needless to say, this may be an instance where reimagining should involve the creation of safe boundaries. Expression and suppression is another interesting tension among conditional forgivers (Kloeber, 2011; Kloeber & Waldron, 2017).

A more recent iteration of relational dialectics theory, called RDT 2.0, provides a critical framework for considering how micro interactions (proximal) between relational partners are influenced by macro (distal) discourses (Baxter, 2011; Baxter et al., 2015). For instance, a couple actively practicing religion and trying to recover from infidelity may have conversations about lying, betrayal, rebuilding trust, apologizing, and offering restitution, embedded within the larger context of scripture and fellowship that encourage forgiveness and reconciliation. Couples may also receive implicit cultural messages from other sources such as family or friends that may sound like, "I'm a failure if I can't make this marriage last" or "Be independent. You don't need a man to be happy."

Making Sense by Attributing Blame

Another common method of making sense of our relational pain is to blame our "guilty" partner. Humans are interpretive animals that make attributions in order to predict and respond to the world around them (Manusov & Spitzberg, 2008). Relationally, when our partners act in ways that catch our attention, we assess the meaning of this behavior in order to know how to best respond. Often this process centers on determining responsibility (Manusov, 2018) – is my partner answerable for how she or he behaved? Weiner (1985) argues that behaviors can be attributed to internal (dispositional) characteristics or external (circumstantial) characteristics. In long-term relationships, internal attributions ("You did this because it is your essential character") regarding negative behavior may result in what has been termed *distress-maintaining attributions* (Manusov & Spitzberg, 2008). These attributions maintain relationship distress because they create a relational frame, or perspective, that the partner is unable, or at least unwilling, to change (Kelley, 2017). These perceptions may create a sense of relational hopelessness and work against imagining a happier future together. In contrast, we can choose relationship enhancing attributions through empathy and imagination.

Empathy and Imagination: Rehumanizing the Other

As we have just described, sense-making can be destructive when it becomes a trap of distress-maintaining attributions. Manusov (2015) suggests that attribution-making "comes at a cost" (p. 197). In contrast to searching for cause and responsibility, she suggests that there are significant benefits to practicing mindfulness in personal relationships, focusing on being present with others, without judgment. This sort of connection between partners is at the heart of Worthington's (2006) suggestion that empathy provides a constructive way of relational sense-making.

When practicing empathy, one shifts from assessing blame to understanding the offending partner's experience and, as Worthington notes, this will "usually lead the victim to see that the offender thought himself or herself to be attacked, threatened, or provoked" (p. 74), and opens the possibility of responding with compassion toward the perceived offender. Broome (2015) echoes this perspective, suggesting that empathy provides a means for predicting other's thoughts, feelings, and behaviors and, as such, helps one make decisions about competent, appropriate responses.

Empathy has been conceptualized as having cognitive, emotion, and behavior-based components (Levenson & Ruef, 1992; Worthington, 2006), such that one knows what one's partner is feeling, feels something akin to what he or she is experiencing, and responds compassionately (behavior intended to relieve the suffering of another). Empathy differs from sympathy, which involves feelings of concern, pity, or care rather than understanding and experiencing the emotions of one's partner (Worthington, 2006). In short, empathy is feeling or thinking *with* the other person, as opposed to feeling sorry *for* him or her.

Empathy has been central to many intervention-based approaches to forgiveness and reconciliation. The consistent relationship between empathy and various aspects of the forgiveness process is likely due to its ability to engender one's imagination, putting oneself in the place of the person who did the hurting or whom you hurt. Research by M. H. Davis (1980; 1983; Pulos, Elison, & Lennon, 2004) emphasizes imagination as a central aspect of empathy. For Davis, empathy is associated with perspective-taking (the tendency to adopt the psychological perspective of others), empathic concern (assesses other-oriented feelings and concern for unfortunate others), personal distress (experience of anxiety and unease in tense interpersonal settings), and fantasy (tendency to imaginatively transpose oneself into the feelings and actions of fictitious others). This multidimensional perspective ties empathy to processes that typically involve imagination – perspective-taking, empathic concern, and fantasy – and suggests that personal distress may inhibit these processes.

Empathy and imagination stand in contradiction to distress-maintaining attributions commonly made by dissatisfied couples. The former is humanizing, whereas the latter dehumanizes one's partner. This is evident in perspectives that characterize human beings as naturally able to adapt and exhibit resilience (Masten, 2001). In this sense, we dehumanize others when we treat them as though they lack an ability to change in response to life's shifting contingencies (Oelofsen, 2009). For example, simple statements during an argument, "You are just like your father!" or "Your entire family is this way", reflect distress-maintaining attributions that imply there is little hope for change (your father never changed; your entire family continues to pass down this fatal flaw). In contrast to dehumanizing attributions and blame, empathy and understanding have the ability to rehumanize our partners. Through imagination we shift our relationship frame, modifying the dehumanizing perspective of our partner ("You hurt me, you animal!"), to one that is human, once again ("You hurt me, but you are also someone who has been in pain") (Kelley, 2017). Oelofsen writes that imagination can be a form of empathy and, significantly, "Imagination can play a role in rehumanizing the other, through enabling an overcoming of indifference to the other's pains and plights" (p. 183). In this way, sense-making becomes the rehumanization of one's partners, an essentially moral perspective that results in the creation of collaborative relational spaces wherein a just futures are possible.

Self-Forgiveness: Rehumanizing the Self

As we have seen, dehumanizing one's partner can result in the creation of a relational space bereft of hope for a joint future. In the same regard, dehumanizing the self, living with a deep sense of shame over one's actions or inactions, potentially limits one's ability to rebuild a positive relationship future with one's partner. In this sense, self-forgiveness is largely a process of sense-making, of reassessing one's identity. Self-forgiveness is not simply needed to alleviate feeling badly about one's own actions, self-forgiveness is needed when one's actions are discordant with one's sense of self. Although self-forgiveness has much in common with interpersonal forgiveness processes, in relation to oneself, the task of forgiveness has some special challenges.

Self-forgiveness has been described as, "a willingness to abandon self-resentment in the face of one's own acknowledged wrong, while fostering compassion, generosity, and love toward oneself" (Enright & the Human Development Study Group, 1996, p. 115). Luskin (2002) fleshes out this definition by describing four categories of self-forgiveness: Frustration at oneself for failing to fulfill one of life's important tasks (e.g., graduating from college or having children); upset at oneself for not acting when presumed necessary (to help oneself or others); disheartened over having hurt someone (e.g., regret over poor parenting or an affair); and lamenting self-destructive acts (e.g., alcohol abuse).

Tangney, Boone, and Dearing (2005) suggest that clients, clinicians, and clergy take care that this process does not become overly self-focused, instead of focusing on a positive future of personal and relational growth. In this vein, Fisher and Exline (2010) suggest that shame, and excessive guilt and regret, may indeed inhibit a healthy, future-focused, self-forgiveness as they may be associated with, "aggression, defensiveness, or self-hatred rather than reparative behaviors" (p. 556). They go on to state, "The key seems to be finding ways to accept responsibility for one's offenses without lapsing into extreme negative emotions that take energy away from the important tasks of relational repair and personal growth."

Luskin (2002) encourages forgivers (self or other) to move toward personal growth by taking things less personally (e.g., understanding we all make mistakes), taking responsibility for their actions (e.g., stop blaming others), and learning to tell positive intention stories (e.g., remembering one's deep desires that underlie the offense – a hope for connection or healing or stability). Luskin's (2002) HEAL method for self-forgiving is a tangible way of embracing these principles. Consider the HEAL method in light of Maddi's hurt feelings when Keisha spoke honestly to her. *H* stands for *hope*, and reminds the self-forgiver of what they hoped for when the transgression occurred: Keisha remembers, "I hoped to be a good, honest friend." *E* represents the importance of *educating* oneself that things do not always happen the way we initially hope: Keisha educates herself that every hope may fail, at times, and accepts the uncertainty that comes with that statement. *A* is the *affirmation* of her positive intention to speak honestly to Maddi, because she cares for Maddi: Keisha quits "beating herself up" for what she said, and remembers that even though her words could have been spoken more gently, her intent was to care for Maddi and speak honestly about some of her life choices. Finally, *L* represents *long-term commitment* and may include acting or learning new skills to avoid the transgression in the future: Keisha decides to apologize to Maddi and ask her how she could better express her ideas next time she has concerns.

Making Sense of Sense-Making

Sense-making is a messy process that takes time and, typically, many iterations of making sense of complex situations. In fact, at the times when we are seeking to end relational turbulence and reduce uncertainty, we would be wise to be wary of overly quick or overly simplistic conclusions to most of our relationship struggles. One reason to avoid quick judgment is that information often continues to surface as the problem is dealt with ("I know I said it was okay, but if I'm totally honest . . ."). Another reason is to allow time for the complex, essential, relationship between emotion and thinking to do its work. Our interviews with couples discovered that individuals often enter a cycle of experiencing emotion and meaning-making – certain emotions trigger certain thoughts which trigger certain emotions . . . These cycles should not be rushed. While individuals may find themselves stuck in sequences where rumination, negative thoughts, and negative feelings feed off of one another (Kachadourian, Fincham, & Davila, 2005; Ysseldyk, Matheson, & Anisman, 2007), the constructive integration of emotional experience and cognitive sense-making forms a foundation from which to move forward with one's life and one's relationships, and is an essential aspect of our human experience.

References

Afifi, W. A., & Weiner, J. L. (2004). Toward a theory of motivated information management. *Communication Theory, 14*, 167–190.

Baxter, L. A. (2003). A tale of two voices: Relational dialectics theory. *Journal of Family Communication, 4*, 181–192.

Baxter, L. A. (2011). *Voicing relationships: A dialogic perspective.* Los Angeles, CA: Sage.

Baxter, L. A., & Montgomery, B. M. (1996). *Relating: Dialogues and dialectics.* New York, NY: Guilford.

Baxter, L. A., Pederson, S. N., & Norwood, K. M. (2015). Negotiating relational morality: Poetic justice. In V. R. Waldron & D. L. Kelley (Eds.), *Moral talk across the lifespan* (pp. 117–135). New York, NY: Peter Lang.

Baxter, L. A., & West, L. (2003). Couple perceptions of their similarities and differences: A dialectical perspective. *Journal of Social and Personal Relationships, 20*, 491–514.

Berger, C. R., & Calabrese, R. (1975). Some explanations in initial interaction and beyond. *Human Communication Research, 1*, 99–112.

Berger, C. R., & Kellerman, K. (1994). Acquiring social information. In J. Daly & J. Weimann (Eds.), *Strategic interpersonal communication* (pp. 1–32). Hillsdale, NJ: Lawrence Erlbaum.

Brashers, D. E. (2001). Communication and uncertainty management. *Journal of Communication, 51*, 447–498.

Broome, B. J. (2015). Empathy. In *The SAGE encyclopedia of intercultural communication*. doi:10.4135/9781483346267.n101

Davis, M. H. (1980). A multidimensional approach to individual differences in empathy. *JSAS Catalog of Selected Documents in Psychology, 10*, 85.

Davis, M. H. (1983). Measuring individual differences in empathy: Evidence for a multidimensional approach. *Journal of Personality and Social Psychology, 44*, 113–126.

Enright, R. D., & the Human Development Study Group. (1991). The moral development of forgiveness. In W. Kurtines & J. Gerwitz (Eds.), *Handbook of moral behavior development* (pp. 123–152). Hillsdale, NJ: Lawrence Erlbaum.

Feeney, J. A. (2005). Hurt feelings in couple relationships: Exploring the role of attachment and perceptions of personal injury. *Personal Relationships, 12*, 253–271.

Fisher, M. L., & Exline, J. J. (2010). *Moving toward self-forgiveness: Removing barriers related to shame, guilt, and regret*. Oxford, UK. doi:10.1111/j.1751–9004.2010.00276.x

Kachadourian, L. K., Fincham, F., & Davila, J. (2005). Attitudinal ambivalence, rumination, and forgiveness of partner transgressions in marriage. *Personality and Social Psychology Bulletin, 31*, 334–342.

Kelley, D. L. (2012). *Marital communication*. Cambridge, UK: Polity Press.

Kelley, D. L. (2017). *Just relationships: Living out social justice as mentor, family, friend, and lover*. New York, NY: Routledge.

Kelley, D. L., & Waldron, V. R. (2005). An investigation of forgiveness-seeking communication and relational outcomes. *Communication Quarterly, 53*, 339–358.

Kloeber, D. N. (2011). *Voicing conditional forgiveness*. Tempe: Arizona State University.

Kloeber, D. N., & Waldron, V. R. (2017). Expressing and suppressing conditional forgiveness in serious romantic relationships. In J. Samp (Ed.), *Communicating interpersonal conflict in close relationships: Contexts, challenges, and opportunities* (pp. 227–249). New York, NY: Routledge.

Knobloch, L. K., Solomon, D. H., Theiss, J. A., & McLaren, R. M. (2018). Relational turbulence theory: Understanding family communication during times of change. In D. Braithwaite, E. Suter, & K. Floyd (Eds.), *Engaging theories of family communication* (2nd ed., pp. 255–266). New York, NY: Taylor & Francis.

Levenson, R. W., & Ruef, A. M. (1992). Empathy: A physiological substrate. *Journal of Personality and Social Psychology, 63*, 234–246.

Luskin, F. (2002). *Forgive for good*. San Francisco, CA: HarperCollins.

Manusov, V. (2015). Mindfulness as morality: Awareness, nonjudgment, and nonreactivity in couples' communication. In V. R. Waldron & D. L. Kelley (Eds.), *Moral talk across the lifespan* (pp. 183–201). New York, NY: Peter Lang.

Manusov, V. (2018). Attribution theory: Who's at fault in families? In D. Braithwaite, E. Suter, & K. Floyd (Eds.), *Engaging theories of family communication* (2nd ed., pp. 51–61). New York, NY: Taylor & Francis.

Manusov, V., & Spitzberg, B. (2008). Attribution theory: Finding good cause in the search for theory. In L. A. Baxter & D. O. Braithwaite (Eds.), *Engaging theories in interpersonal communication: Multiple perspectives* (pp. 37–49). Los Angeles, CA: Sage.

Masten, A. S. (2001). Ordinary magic: Resilience processes in development. *American Psychologist, 56*(3), 227–238. doi:10.1037/0003–066X.56.3.227

Merolla, A. J., & Zhang, S. (2011). In the wake of transgressions: Examining forgiveness communication in personal relationships. *Personal Relationship, 18*(1), 79–95. doi:10.1111/j.1475–6811.2010.01323.x

Oelofsen, R. (2009). De- and rehumanization in the wake of atrocities. *South African Journal of Philosophy, 28*(2), 178–188. doi:10.4314/sajpem.v28i2.46677

Pulos, S., Elison, J., & Lennon, R. (2004). The hierarchical structure of the Interpersonal Reactivity Index. *Social Behavior and Personality, 32*, 355–359.

Schwary, R. L. (Producer), & Redford, R. (Director). (1980). *Ordinary people* [Motion picture]. US: Paramount Pictures.

Solomon, D. H., & McLaren, R. M. (2008). Relational framing theory: Drawing inferences about relationships from interpersonal interactions. In L. A. Baxter & D. O. Braithwaite (Eds.), *Engaging theories in interpersonal communication: Multiple perspectives* (pp. 103–115). Thousand Oaks, CA: Sage.

Tangney, J. P., Boone, A. L., & Dearing, R. (2005). Forgiving the self: Conceptual issues and empirical findings. In E. L. Worthington, Jr. (Ed.), *Handbook of forgiveness* (pp. 143–158). New York, NY: Routledge.

TED. (2012, May 19). *Walid Afifi: How uncertainty affects us (and five simple words to make a change)* [Video file]. Retrieved from https://youtube.com/watch?v=GFLtl70rB7g

Waldron, V. R., & Kelley, D. (2005). Forgiveness as a response to relational transgression. *Journal of Social and Personal Relationships, 22*, 723–742.

Waldron, V. R., & Kelley, D. L. (2008). *Communicating forgiveness.* Thousand Oaks, CA: Sage.

Weiner, B. (1996). Searching for order in social motivation. *Psychological Inquiry, 7*(3), 199–216. doi:10.1207/s15327965pli0703_1

Worthington, E. L., Jr. (2006). *Forgiveness and reconciliation: Theory and application.* New York, NY: Routledge.

Yoshimura, S. M., & Boon, S. D. (2018). *Communicating revenge in interpersonal relationships.* Lanham, MD: Lexington Books.

Ysseldyk, R., Matheson, K., & Anisman, H. (2007). Rumination: Bridging a gap between forgivingness, vengefulness, and psychological health. *Personality and Individual Differences, 42*(8), 1573–1584.

PART III

Remaking Our Relationships

Personal and Community Applications

6

FORGIVENESS

Reimagining Our Response to Personal Pain

My mother wrote a long letter to me then, reminding me of the special bond she had expected to share with me, her first born son, how she had opened her heart to me throughout her life, how she had raised me like a prince, sacrificed for me, lived for me. She reminded me of the sins of her enemy, her brother-in-law. How he had allowed us to nearly starve in Chongqing without lifting a finger to help us. . . . She could never forgive this act of betrayal, my mother wrote; I was no longer her son. – Winberg Chai recounting his mother's response after he had visited his dying uncle, her brother-in-law, who his mother considered her enemy.

★

Reimagining Our Relationships has explored elements related to the inevitability of change, the murky arena of experiencing emotions and managing their effects, and post-transgression sense-making, with specific emphasis on processes that rehumanize each partner in the relationship. At this point, we make the critical move of examining how these elements may work together to bring about interpersonal forgiveness. Forgiveness, when engaged in a healthy manner, brings the emotional and relational healing necessary to fully reimagine and rebuild positive, constructive relationships.

Consider the opening quotation of this chapter. Winberg Chai (2001) describes his mother's response after he secretly visited his dying uncle, her "enemy" that "she could never forgive". The sense of betrayal, experienced by Chai's mother, is clear. Equally evident is how experiencing emotion and unilaterally assigning meaning to a hurtful situation can feel incomplete, to one or both relational partners. Missing is reimagination. The *Model of Relationship Reimagination* (see *Chapter 2*) suggests that hurting partners talk themselves into positive emotional, perceptual, and behavioral *change* regarding self, other, and the relationship. Because this process is prompted by painful relationship experience and experienced as (im)moral in nature, it is often forgiveness that provides the necessary means to accomplish the rather grandiose aim of creating a new future. The following discussion examines various perspectives on forgiveness, takes a look at potential dark sides of forgiving, and offers *imaginative forgiveness* as a constructive response to relationship harm. We begin by examining various *forgiveness quandaries*.

The Essential Forgiveness Quandary

Throughout our relational histories we find ourselves in what might be called the *essential forgiveness quandary*:

> hurt persons desire release from their pain, yet . . . forgiveness is made difficult by experience of the very pain it is designed to alleviate, and forgiving the offense seemingly perpetuates the very injustice which is the source of the pain itself.

This quandary is a natural manifestation of the emotional trauma and cognitive uncertainty present during relationship transgression, pain, and change. Individuals report, "I'm too angry to forgive" or "I'm afraid that if I forgive I will be condoning the 'bad' behavior, and it will never stop". These are legitimate issues that have fostered significant dialogue and debate across various contexts of human pain and suffering. Here we briefly explore four contexts where the appropriateness of forgiveness has been debated: Response to historical trauma, philosophical search for meaning, religious foci on reconciliation, and pursuit of psychological and relational well-being.

Forgiveness and Trauma

Besides the moral concern that characterizes all forgiveness quandaries (if we forgive, this injustice can happen again), historical trauma is problematic because of its sheer magnitude (how can you possibly forgive genocide?). Yet, there is a need to pursue justice without remaining shackled to the past. World figures as diverse as Simon Wiesenthal and Desmond Tutu have grappled with this tension. A poignant example is provided in *The Sunflower: On the Possibilities and Limits of Forgiveness* (Wiesenthal, 2008). Here, Wiesenthal recounts a personal event where he, imprisoned as a Jew, was asked to forgive a young, dying, Nazi SS officer's crimes against the Jewish people. At the end of his story, Wiesenthal encourages the reader to change mental places with him, struggling with the quandary, "What would I have done?" (p. 98). In the second part of the book, political and religious leaders, writers and social activists, and other survivors of genocide respond to Wiesenthal's query. Of these responses, only 12 espouse forgiveness, 16 are opposed to it, and 25 express ambivalence. Themes in respondents' essays represent such forgiveness challenges as defining forgiveness, examining the process and functions of forgiveness, and exploring possible conditions and dark sides of forgiveness (Goman & Kelley, 2016).

Desmond Tutu, in his book *No Future Without Forgiveness* (1999), makes the direct argument that forgiveness is needed to create a positive future. To this end, he examines the South African Government's quandary as to how to respond in a just manner to apartheid trauma, while also taking action that would be constructive for the country's future. Tutu recounts how truth and reconciliation commissions were created to deal with the tension of providing some degree of both justice and forgiveness for victims and perpetrators in an effort to help the country move forward from deep division and violence. In both of these books, each author struggles with the quandary of how to offer a healthy form of forgiveness that is not "cheap" or counter-productive, as well as the potential problems of not forgiving – nurtured anger and bitterness reinforcing long-held separation and strife. In addition, both recognize the need for justice, as well as the impossibility of ever achieving complete justice for the atrocities experienced.

Forgiveness and the Philosophical Search for Meaning

Forgiveness as a philosophical topic is equally challenging. Arendt (1958) expresses the dilemma of forgiveness as, "Men are unable to forgive what they cannot punish and . . . they are unable to punish what has turned out to be unforgiveable" (p. 241). This process creates a potential cycle of despair, or despondency. In our studies, we have found many people more able to forgive once the offender has experienced consequences for her or his actions (e.g., punishment). Yet, not all offenses are punishable in a way that feels satisfactory. Nussbaum (2016) suggests that we err in our judgment when we are, "focusing on what this offender 'deserves' rather than on the larger issue of human well-being and how to protect it" (p. 179).

Interestingly, the current surge in interest about forgiveness (Nussbaum, 2016) may reflect a general societal shift in how forgiveness, and human experience, is understood. Griswold (2007) emphasizes how understandings of forgiveness have morphed in response to the general move to emphasize equality in human relations. He notes that modern perspectives on forgiveness differ from ancient viewpoints in the sense that we see each other as equals, mutually dependent on one another. Philosopher Joanna North (1987, 1998) pushes this envelope even farther, creating new forgiveness quandaries as she suggests forgiveness may actually include a loving response toward the offender. This echoes Arendt's (1958) belief that forgiveness frees the offender to change, no longer trapped in the past:

"Without being forgiven, released from the consequences of what we have done, our capacity to act would, as it were, be confined to one single deed from which we could never recover; we would remain the victims of its consequences forever . . ." (p. 237).

Forgiveness and Religious Emphasis on Reconciliation

As communication scholars, religious aspects of forgiveness have been particularly interesting to us because faith perspectives typically situate forgiveness as a response to moral transgression, within a relationship context ("Love your enemies" – Jesus, Matthew 5:44; The Dalai Lama, 1997/2003). Yet, a key quandary for many religions is negotiating the perceived struggle between mercy and justice. For example, as we write this section of the book, forgiveness has come crashing into the news as the United States made moves to normalize relationships with Cuba. Archbishop Jaime Lucas Ortega told President Obama that forgiveness will be necessary because history is the essence of life and "cannot be easily forgotten" (Ravsberg, 2016). Ortega's statement emphasizes the tensions between the desire for healing, justice, and reconciliation.

The notion of forgiveness surfaces in certain early Hindu and Buddhist texts, and the sacred scriptures and writings for each of the Abrahamic faiths (Judaism, Christianity, Islam) emphasize the centrality of forgiveness as a means of reconciliation between God and humankind (Rye et al., 2000), and between people. Yet, much religious thought tries, in some way, to understand the relationship between justice and mercy. Volf (2001), for example, examines problems with the principle of *first justice, then reconciliation*, by claiming that it leaves conflicting parties "at odds" with each other, is actually not desirable (e.g., would any of us truly want to return to a way of living that is "an eye for an eye"), and most essentially, is impossible to achieve. Instead, Volf argues for the *will to embrace*, even embracing the offender as human. Volf's admonition to embrace echoes thoughts from religious leaders as diverse as Jesus, "If you love those who love you, what benefit is that to you? For even sinners love those who love them. . . . But love your enemies," and Hanh (2014), "When there is no more blame or criticism in your eyes, when you are able to look at others with compassion . . . the other person can sense you are truly seeing her and understanding her" (pp. 38, 39).

Forgiveness and Psychological and Relational Well-Being

Feeling "wronged" presents additional forgiveness quandaries as related to personal health and well-being. Even though many of us believe in the benefits of "letting go" of one's bitterness and anger, there can be something empowering about staying angry. Truth be told, many of us would rather stay angry when wronged than offer mercy and let the offending person "off the hook".

Forgiveness is at times a process of overriding certain emotional responses or desires, and choosing personal and relational health. As one of our research participants stated,

> Therapists say you don't have to forgive in the beginning, you have to work at it. Well, I learned you could forgive in the beginning. Even if you just mouth it in your heart. There is something to saying "I forgive you . . ." And then you start building on that and actually the person doing the forgiving is the one that gets the gift.
>
> (Waldron & Kelley, 2008, p. 63)

This wife obviously has been encouraged to take time to forgive, yet, she finds great comfort in choosing to begin the process. Undoubtedly this was a complicated effort in decision making. Throughout our research we've noticed that even when convinced that forgiveness is good for our own psychological well-being, it is not easy to choose forgiveness as a response to relational pain. When Doug was in counseling with his wife Ann, he was surprised at how hard forgiveness was (even though he had been teaching about it for two decades!). Truth be told, there were times when he preferred to hold on to his hurt and anger, rather than heal his relationship, and himself.

Many individuals recognize that harboring negative emotions for long periods of time is not good for one's mental or physical states and yet letting go of negative emotions through forgiveness may seem unfair and to run the risk of the "victims" re-victimizing themselves. Also, classic conflict management strategies may fall short when what has happened to us, or what we have done to someone else, seems "wrong" or "bad" or we simply can't fathom that this actually "happened to me". Common emotional responses to infidelity, for example, include anger, vulnerability, shock, and embarrassment (Guerrero & Cole, 2015), in large part because the wrongdoing is not simply a setback in one's relational goals, but involves a violation of the relationship's moral rules or guidelines – "honesty above all else", "no dating other people or hooking up at parties".

A consistent struggle with forgiving in personal relationships (and, as we've seen, in other contexts, such as historical trauma) is the perception that it undermines our sense of relational justice. More forgiveness-reticent individuals are often slow to express forgiveness because it doesn't seem "fair". Their feelings and thoughts could be expressed something like: "After you broke our relationship understanding (e.g., rules, guidelines, norms), and put me through emotional hell, I'm just supposed to forgive you and let things get back to normal? I don't think so." Our respondents have also expressed the concern that, if they forgive, the offender will fail to experience consequences to her or his actions, or it will send a message that the wrongdoing can happen again without consequence.

All that said, there is a significant amount of work demonstrating the health benefits of forgiveness and forgiveness-related processes (Kelley, Wolf, & Broberg,

2016; Toussaint, Worthington, & Williams, 2015). A significant volume on the subject explores potential forgiveness benefits related to physical and mental health, most specifically related to chronic pain, substance abuse, and its role in facilitating well-being and aging, culture, and personal relationships (Toussaint et al., 2015). Kelley et al. (2016) summarize these benefits:

> Forgiveness, and/or the moderation of unforgiveness, is associated with the exhibition of positive affect (e.g., sympathy, empathy, and optimism), improved self-esteem, higher life satisfaction, and better mental health ratings. Physical health effects of forgiveness include enhanced bioregulation in response to transgression stressors, as well as better self-rated health status and the exhibition of positive health behaviors.
>
> (p. 1)

For our purposes, it is most essential to recognize that various elements related to the forgiveness process have been consistently associated with relational well-being (Davis, Green, Reid, Moloney, & Burnette, 2015; Fincham, 2015; Worthington, 2006). In light of this evidence suggesting that "forgiveness likely influences relationship health and vice versa" (Fincham, 2015, p. 261), we move on to an examination of various interpersonally based forgiveness models and end the chapter by offering a perspective that depicts forgiveness as an imaginative process. However, before discussing specific forgiveness models, we address issues raised by a number of authors regarding potential negative consequences to forgiving.

Potential Dark Sides of Forgiveness

A number of authors have written about potential dark sides of forgiveness (Enright, Eastin, Golden, Sarinopoulos, & Freedman, 1992; McNulty, 2011). The "dark side" references potentially negative personal or relationship outcomes associated with forgiving. This dark line of thinking is generally aimed at dispelling the "myth" that forgiveness is a panacea for managing personal pain and suffering and suggests that, worse, it may even contribute to negative relational or personal/psychological experience of forgiver and forgive alike.

An example of this perspective is provided by McNulty (2011), who argues that forgiveness works in opposition to well-established psychological theories, such as operant conditioning, which suggests that "people are less likely to repeat existing patterns of behavior only if those behaviors are followed by unwanted outcomes" (p. 771). His longitudinal study with newlywed couples found that spouses who reported more of a tendency to express forgiveness saw stable patterns of verbal and physical violence in their relationships over four years, whereas those spouses less willing to forgive experienced a reduction in violence.

McNulty's (2011) work demonstrates the importance of understanding the forgiveness process before engaging it with relational partners. For instance, as we discuss in the following section in this chapter, a number of concepts are often confused with forgiveness, such as excusing, justifying, or tolerating bad behavior. Even more problematic is the potentially dangerous idea that forgiveness demands reconciliation, whether or not the offending party is a safe person (psychologically and physically) with whom to be in relationship. Another problematic notion is the belief that forgiveness removes any personal or relational negative consequence. In healthy forgiving situations, the natural consequences of one's actions may take years to dissipate. For example, rebuilding trust after an extra-relational affair may take years.

The problem of lay persons conceptualizing forgiveness in ways that are potentially hurtful is not just a problem for forgivers and offenders, it is a shortcoming of much forgiveness research (including our own!) that lets individuals self-define forgiveness. This type of "self-defined" research results in participants responding to questions, such as, "How likely are you to forgive?" or "How do you forgive?", based on their own conceptualizations of forgiveness. Research targeting these "lay" conceptualizations of forgiveness has uncovered numerous discrepancies between what is commonly thought about forgiveness and how scholars tend to conceptualize it. For instance, common perceptions of forgiveness include reconciliation as a central component, as well as "forgetting" (Kearns & Fincham, 2004), whereas forgiveness researchers tend to take great pains in order to distinguish forgiveness from these concepts. The point here is that negative outcomes of forgiveness, emerging from certain social science-based research studies, may in part be a function of participants' "unhealthy" conceptualizations of how to forgive.

Related, negative relationship consequences have been associated with what has been termed conditional forgiveness. Conditional forgiveness is represented by *forgiveness if* – I will forgive you . . . if there is behavior change, if there is restitution, if there are no more mistakes. As one of our respondents stated to her alcoholic father, "I told him I would accept his apology, however, we both knew that there was the stipulation that he stay off the booze." Although conditional forgiveness may serve certain positive functions (e.g., productive boundary setting, especially when conditions are expressed rather than hidden), researchers are still uncertain why conditional forgiveness has consistently been associated with negative relational outcomes. Some have suggested that conditional forgiveness is not "real" forgiveness because it is not given unconditionally (Derrida, 2001; Enright, 2001). Research by Kloeber (2011) discovered that often when individuals report that they have conditionally forgiven, what they actually have done is placed conditions on how to reconcile or rebuild the relationship. It is possible that this confusion regarding forgiveness and reconciliation is responsible for many associated negative outcomes. Others have proposed that conditional forgiveness creates a power imbalance in the relationship that is destructive

(Kloeber & Waldron, 2017). For instance "I will *only* forgive you if . . ." restricts the choices of one relational partner by the other. The resulting power imbalance may lead the diminished partner to pull away from the relationship. A final possibility is that conditions set are unrealistically high. In the previous example, wherein the daughter tells her father that forgiveness is predicated on him "staying off the booze", this expectation may be improbable (though understandable) for someone who has substance abuse problems. In this case, the daughter is likely confusing forgiveness with reconciliation and stipulating conditions that may set up her father for failure. An alternative would be to forgive her father and set boundaries that stipulate that she will only continue in the relationship if he regularly attends a support group, such as Alcoholics Anonymous, in order to change his addictive behaviors. We will come back to the topic of conditional forgiveness later in this chapter, and unpack the controversy much more fully in *Chapter 7: Reconciliation: Imagining a New Future*, but for now it is sufficient to understand that while conditional forgiveness may provide positive outcomes, such as protecting oneself from additional emotional harm, it can potentially have some dark consequences.

The dark-side examples we have provided here highlight how individuals who see or experience negative personal and relational outcomes from forgiveness often define or enact forgiveness in ways that are unhealthy or destructive. Philosopher Joanna North (1998) reminds us that forgiveness has to "occur in the right way and for the right reasons" (p. 20). Essentially, when our forgiveness practice comes from unhealthy motivations (e.g., maintain our own co-dependence), we run the risk of damaging our relationships, our partners, and ourselves. As such, we turn our attention to conceptual distinctions between forgiveness and not-forgiveness concepts, existing interpersonal-based forgiveness models, and introduce a definition of *imaginative forgiveness* that we believe is healing, constructive, and redemptive.

What Is Not-Forgiveness

In our experience, many people who claim "I don't do forgiveness" are actually rejecting a perspective of forgiveness that most researchers also reject. Following, we discuss a sampling of concepts that either misrepresent forgiveness or, as we saw in the preceding section, can be damaging because they offer a limited or simplistic perspective on forgiveness.

Simple Apology

We begin with simple apology because *apology* (and acceptance of apology) is often considered, by lay individuals, synonymous with forgiveness (Waldron & Kelley, 2008). For many of us, our early forgiveness training was learning to say "I'm sorry". However, forgiveness can be accomplished without apology, and apology can be manipulative. For example, one of our students, Josiah, reported that after he and his father had a "huge blowup" his father would apologize to him, but then say, "And . . .", waiting for Josiah to reciprocate the apology. Josiah went on to discuss how those experiences left him thinking that forgiveness was manipulative. Another way apology may misrepresent the forgiveness process is when apology is used as an avoidance tactic. Savvy communicators may quickly apologize to avoid having to talk about the nuances of a sticky situation. All that said, it is important to recognize that apology is a critical component of imaginative reconciliation, and later in the text we discuss how to actually offer an apology that has benefits for both partners and the relationship as a whole.

Forgetting

Along with "say you're sorry", the maxim "forgive and forget" may sum up the extent of most people's forgiveness repertoire. However, the juxtaposition of forgetting and forgiving is problematic. First, victims generally cannot forget painful experiences, even when they want to. Forgetting is not a simple act of the will. Second, forgetting implies that moral violations have been overlooked, that lessons learned from the incident may have been forgotten. In fact, active acknowledgment of the transgression may be the factor that most distinguishes forgiveness from related concepts such as condoning, excusing, and denying. When individuals say "Can we just forgive and forget?", often what they actually desire is a *pragmatic forgetting* whereby the offended partner ceases to bring up the hurtful event during conversation or conflict.

Excusing, Justifying, and Condoning

Researchers are virtually unanimous that excusing, justifying, and condoning are not acts of forgiveness. All of these responses, in one way or another, fail to recognize or deal with an offense. For example, excusing reframes the offense so that it is no longer seen as a moral infraction. Justification provides "good reasons" for the offensive behavior so the offender is free from responsibility. And condoning looks to outside circumstances to accept why the offense happened, yet leaves the offended party viewed negatively (Enright & Fitzgibbons, 2000). Interestingly, these are appropriate responses, at times, and are often confused with forgiveness because they may actually reduce unforgiveness (e.g., ruminations focused on bitterness, revenge, or other anti-social responses; Worthington, 2006).

Reconciliation

Distinguishing between forgiveness and reconciliation is critical to reimagining and establishing healthy relationships and partners. In our research and conversations with others we have discovered that a common motivator for resistance to forgiveness is believing that if one forgives, he or she has to continue the relationship with the offender. From this perspective, forgiveness resistance is prudent because reconciliation with a perceived offender may not be safe, wise, or desirable (McCullough, Pargament, & Thoresen, 2000). For example, trying to reconcile with an abusive spouse may place one in a psychologically or physically dangerous situation (Rye, Folck, Heim, Olszewski, & Traina, 2004). Moreover, conceptualizing reconciliation as a required component of forgiveness unnecessarily empowers the offender to stop the forgiveness process, although working through the forgiveness process (without reconciliation) may have substantial benefits for the injured party. Enright and Fitzgibbons (2000) address this issue when they state, "Forgiveness is one person's individual choice to abandon resentment and to adopt friendlier attitudes toward a wrongdoer . . . [It] is a free choice on the part of the one wronged" (p. 41). The practical result of this free choice is that, even though forgiveness is integral to full reconciliation, the wounded party may choose to discontinue the relationship, even though "friendlier attitudes" have developed – in essence, *choosing to forgive, but not to reconcile*.

Psychological and Therapeutic Perspectives on Forgiveness

There has been an explosion of therapeutically-based forgiveness writing and research over that past three decades, beginning with early work by Enright and colleagues (Enright, Gassin, & Wu, 1992). Most of this work can be characterized as intrapsychic, interventionist (therapeutic), or interpersonal (Worthington, 2005).

McCullough et al. (2000) conceptualize forgiveness as psychosocial in that it is, "intraindividual, prosocial change toward a perceived transgressor that is situated within a specific interpersonal context" (p. 9) and provides a solid foundation from which to build an understanding of forgiveness and reconciliation. Blending psychological and social perspectives allows for a focus on intraindividual experience (e.g., emotion in response to a relational transgression) and cognitive response (e.g., sense-making and subsequent decision-making), as well as examination of prosocial behaviors within relational contexts (e.g., apology, granting forgiveness, and renegotiating the relationship).

Five characteristics have emerged in most psychological conceptualizations of forgiveness (Tucker, Bitman, Wade, & Cornish, 2013). First, a distinguishing characteristic of forgiveness is recognition of an offense, plus an accompanying initial emotional response (e.g., anger, vulnerability, shock, embarrassment; Guerrero & Cole, 2015). Second, the continuation of negative thoughts and emotions in reaction to the offensive behavior. Third, recognition that previous means of managing the hurt have not worked (e.g., avoidance, distraction, revenge). Fourth, a freely chosen cognitive decision to forgive. Fifth, cognitive, affective, and/or behavioral change of the offended person's response to the offender, typically from negative to positive.

Communication-Based Approaches to Forgiveness

How forgiveness is communicated has been the focus of other researchers, including ourselves. Merolla (2017) highlights common communication aspects of interpersonal forgiveness by focusing on self-presentation, relational negotiation, and meaning created through social construction over time. These communication elements are evident in Waldron and Kelley's (2008) *Communication Tasks of Forgiveness* (*CTF*; see Box 6.1). The *CTF* begins with the task of *confront the transgression*. As we previously discussed, without recognition that something "wrong" or hurtful happened, forgiveness does not take place. Common communication tactics at this part of the process include questions, probing, requests for information, confession, self-disclosure, and truth-telling. Second and third tasks entail *managing emotions* triggered by the transgression discovery and attempts to *make sense* of what has happened. This process typically involves emotion regulatory acts such as venting, editing, and expressing one's emotion (*see Chapter 4*), coupled with the sense-making strategies of questioning, probing, observing one's partner's behavior, and seeking information from third parties (*see Chapter 5*). Often these emotional responses and cognitions feed on one another, creating an emotion–cognition cycle. For example, initial emotions associated with discovery of a transgression (hurt, anger, shock) precipitate thoughts regarding oneself ("What's wrong with me?" "Why did this happen to me?") and one's partner ("Is s/he trustworthy?" "Could this happen again?"). Answers to these questions precipitate new emotion-based responses, and so on. Fourth and fifth tasks involve *seeking and granting forgiveness*. Seeking often involves apologizing, expressing regret, and making amends, whereas forgiveness-granting verbally and nonverbally extends mercy in some form. Tasks six and seven focus on reemphasizing and *renegotiating relational values and rules* and, then, maintaining this process through the *transition to a new stabilized relationship*.

How We Communicate Forgiveness

As one would guess, the process of seeking forgiveness for wrongs done, and granting forgiveness for hurt endured, is complicated and takes many forms. Work by Waldron and Kelley (Kelley, 1998; Kelley & Waldron, 2005; Waldron & Kelley, 2005, 2008) and Merolla (2008, 2017; Merolla & Zhang, 2011) has focused on the communication of forgiveness, specifically exploring tasks four and five of *CTF* (2008) which emphasize specific forgiveness-seeking and -granting strategies. Following we explore various means by which both offenders and wounded engage the forgiveness process.

BOX 6.1 COMMUNICATION TASKS OF FORGIVENESS (CTF): AN ALTERNATE PRESCRIPTIVE MODEL*

Task 1: Confront the Transgression
One or both parties must acknowledge that wrongdoing has been committed and that at least one partner has been badly hurt. Responsibility for the transgression must be taken and (sometimes) shared.

Task 2: Manage Emotion
Strong negative emotion must be appropriately expressed, labeled, acknowledged, legitimized, accepted, and deintensified. Emotions may include shock, anger and fear among others.

Task 3: Engage in Sense-Making
The wounded invites information-sharing about motives, situational details, and explanations, all in an effort to manage uncertainty and assess the magnitude of the offense. The offender provides an honest explanation. The parties jointly construct the meaning of the offense by considering it in the context of past behavior, current relational understandings, and implications for the future.

Task 4: Seek Forgiveness
The offending partner sincerely apologizes, expresses regret, and (where appropriate) offers to make amends. The forgiver assesses the request for forgiveness, develops empathy, and communicates openness to the possibility of forgiveness.

Task 5: Grant Forgiveness
The wounded partner indicates a willingness to forgive. Forgiveness may be extended immediately and unequivocally or a long-term process may be initiated. To reduce risk, conditional forgiveness may be offered and third parties may be involved.

Task 6: Negotiate Values and Rules
Clarify the values and rules which will govern the relationship during the post-forgiveness period. Renegotiate the "relational covenant". Create the moral structure which ensures fairness and justice in future interactions.

Task 7: Transition: Monitor, Maintain, or Renegotiate
Monitor and maintain relational agreements, build trust, confidence, and hope. Derive meaning from the experience, focus on the future, and consider a redefined relationship if the process fails.

*Modified from Waldron and Kelley (2008).

Seeking Forgiveness

Kelley (1998) found that individuals seek forgiveness in order to restore the relationship or well-being of oneself or one's partner. Using Likert-type scales and open-ended questions with 186 romantic partners, Kelley and Waldron (2005) discovered five strategies commonly used to seek forgiveness. The first, *explicit acknowledgment*, includes acknowledging a wrongful act and most commonly takes the form of apology. Apology is, perhaps, the most obvious of forgiveness-seeking strategies. As discussed previously, simple apology may actually be used to avoid dealing with the consequences of a relationship transgression; however, simple apologies may also be sufficient for minor infractions of norms and rules. It seems most evident that sincere apologies are most satisfying for relational partners (Schumann, 2012).

A second forgiveness-seeking approach is *explanation*. When done well, those who have offended offer information to promote understanding (Foss & Griffin, 1995) and hopefully facilitate empathy in the offended party. Often this process is invitational: "Let's sit and talk about what happened", "I'd like you to hear my side of the story". However, explanation can certainly turn to the dark side when used to manipulate or promote non-forgiveness responses such as excuse and justification. Although there are times when excuse and justification are appropriate (for more on this, explore the "account-making" literature, e.g., Cody & McLaughlin, 1990), these approaches undermine the forgiveness-seeking process.

The third forgiveness-seeking strategy, *nonverbal assurance*, serves a number of different functions, including demonstrating sincerity and face saving. Part of the importance of nonverbal messages in the forgiveness process is that they are commonly relied upon to determine deception. Individuals' reliance on nonverbal behaviors is likely due to a number of factors, including that at times they are more revealing than speech, can be observed when a partner is not speaking, and are often harder to control than speech (Vrij, 2006). These elements may play an important role in assessing an offender's sincerity and honesty when apologizing. Consonant with this, when used in conjunction with explicit acknowledgment and explanation, nonverbal assurance likely bolsters confidence in the offender's character and assuages the fear that the offense will be repeated (Waldron & Kelley, 2008).

Compensation is a fourth means of seeking forgiveness. In many ways compensation is a justice concept. If an offender can do something to restore equity (i.e., justice; Kelley, 2017), or at least symbolically indicate a desire to "make things right", he or she may do so in an effort to stimulate forgiveness on the part of the offended party. The use of equity-based strategies to preserve and maintain relationships has been well established (e.g., Canary & Stafford, 1992). In the aftermath of a transgression, compensation attempts may include concrete responses, such as restitution ("Please let me pay for the damage I did to your car") and gift-giving ("I hope this gift card can help make amends . . ."). However, compensation can take more subtle forms – groveling or being "extra nice" for extended periods of time – that attempt to "pay for" transgressions that are not easily recompensed. These aspects may be coupled with promise as a means of rectifying hurtful behavior ("I've closed my Match account, so I will no longer contact previous dating partners").

The final strategy to emerge in Kelley and Waldron's (2005) work on forgiveness-seeking is humor. When used sparingly, humor can be helpful to manage minor transgressions. When used appropriately, humor can ease heightened states of arousal, allowing partners to gain fresh perspective and engage in fruitful discussion. However, because forgiveness is typically associated with more severe transgressions, humor can be a risky strategy. If an offended party views attempted humor as diversionary, "making light" of a serious offense, or failing to recognize the emotional pain of the transgression, the use of humor may be in need of forgiveness, itself!

Granting Forgiveness

Merolla (2017) compiles a record of 15 communication strategies used to forgive others. These strategies can be understood both in terms of approach (direct or indirect) and potential relational or personal outcomes (healing or threatening) (Kelley, 1998; Merolla, 2017), and may be selected based on the relational and personal goals of the forgiver (to ease personal pain or facilitate reconciliation), as well as the wounded party's perception as to the offender's possible responses. Kelley's (1998) work suggests that possible forgiver goals include a desire to express love, to respond to an offender's forgiveness-seeking actions (e.g., apology), to reframe a transgression event, and to restore the relationship and the well-being of oneself and one's partner.

Merolla (2017) suggests a four-part categorization of forgiveness styles, based on two dimensions: Direct–indirect and healing–threatening. Engaging strategies (direct, healing) include explicitly offering forgiveness, discussion of the transgression, and clear nonverbal indicators of forgiveness. De-emphasizing forgiveness-granting (indirect, healing) is performed through use of humor, downplaying, or "returning to normal". The conditional style (direct, threatening) uses stipulations, demand of debt repayment, or assurances of future behavior change as specifications as to whether forgiveness will be offered or maintained. Suppressing strategies (indirect and threatening) are means of non-expression of forgiveness to the offending party through silence or avoiding discussion, though forgiveness may have taken place intra-psychically for the offended party.

Five forgiveness-granting strategies, identified by Waldron and Kelley (2005), parallel their work on forgiveness-seeking, and overlap with Merolla's typology. The first, and perhaps most obvious of the strategies, *explicit*, is a direct statement that utilizes the word *forgiveness*: "I forgive you" or an equivalent phrase.

The declaration, *I forgive you*, has considerable relational force (Scobie & Scobie, 1998). As a speech act it may convey unconditional pardon or acceptance. Ironically, the raw force of the statement may be the very reason that explicit forgiveness is not offered more frequently. There is a potential loss of face for the offender when told he or she has been forgiven. Interestingly, we observed this phenomenon in our interviews with long-term married couples (Waldron & Kelley, 2008). During joint interviews (both marriage partners were present) participants often protected face for one another, only to reveal potentially hurtful details later in the privacy of the individual interviews that followed. A common sentiment we heard from our couples, when we were interviewing each partner alone, was: "I didn't want to share too much information about the issue when he was present. We've dealt with things and it would just be too painful for him if I brought it up, again." One may also intimate, from this example, that explicitly offering forgiveness, direct as it is, may secondarily function to avoid further discussion regarding the transgression and, thus, to emotionally safeguard either offender or offended party.

The second of Waldron and Kelley's forgiveness-granting strategies is *discussion*. Discussion is the counterpart to using *explanation* to seek forgiveness. Common words and phrases signifying this strategy are, "We talked about it", "We simply discussed the issue and the nature of our relationship", and "understanding" (especially understanding why the transgression occurred). Interestingly, in some regards discussion is a direct strategy (the problem is directly discussed), yet discussion may also serve indirect purposes if partners never explicitly discuss forgiveness. For instance, once an acceptable level of understanding is achieved regarding the transgression and surrounding factors, partners often consider forgiveness to have taken place. This is especially true when discussion includes the third forgiveness-granting strategy, *nonverbal display* of forgiveness. As was the case with forgiveness-seeking, hugs and facial expressions are often used to demonstrate that forgiveness has taken place. Nonverbal display, whether used as a singular strategy or to accompany other strategies, serves both direct and indirect functions of forgiveness. It may save face for the offending party (offering a big hug, rather than stating, "I forgive you"), help the often elusive nature of forgiveness to feel more "real", or, as we discussed previously, add a sense of authenticity to the forgiveness process because certain nonverbal expressions (e.g., tears) are often perceived to be less controllable than words.

A fourth strategy, *minimizing*, is an indirect means of granting forgiveness. Minimizing potentially serves numerous functions as partners redefine the severity of the transgression ("I told them it wasn't a big deal", "I said, 'forget about it'"). Healthier functions include wisely picking your battles, protecting one's partner's face when raising an issue could create undue harm, or maintaining a relationship that is fragile but worth pursuing. Potentially unhealthy functions include regularly avoiding conflict over issues that need to be dealt with and avoidance of healthy negative emotions (Waldron & Kelley, 2005).

A fifth strategy identified by Waldron and Kelley (2005) is conditional forgiveness. Conditional forgiveness can be thought of as *forgiveness if*, and uses some form of condition or stipulation to directly, and explicitly, identify when forgiveness could be withdrawn or ended. Conditions are often set to protect offended parties from further harm, to realign norms in the relationship, and to encourage constructive behaviors by the offender ("I will forgive you if you promise to see a counselor"). If not done with care, these positively intended strategies can be perceived as control attempts.

Relational Forgiveness: An Imaginative Perspective

The myriad forgiveness issues overviewed in this chapter illustrate the complexity of defining forgiveness and, eventually, conceptualizing the forgiveness process. In 2008, we offered a communication-based definition of engaging forgiveness relationally (Waldron & Kelley, 2008). We used a prototype approach to create this definition. Central to a prototype approach is recognition that complex human processes are often "fuzzy" to define (Prager, 1995) – for example, love, family, and friendship are all difficult to define, yet most of us think we know when we see or experience them.

Using our previous definition as a starting point, and taking into consideration the "fuzzy" nature of forgiveness, here we offer an *imaginative* perspective. Forgiveness that embraces imagination includes certain necessary components (necessary to be considered forgiveness; in **bold**, below) and desired components (not always present, but often useful in creating a constructive forgiveness process; in *italics*, below). Most importantly, taking an imaginative approach to relational forgiving opens a pathway to creating a hopeful future by providing healing for past hurts and reconceptualization of one's present. Using this approach, *imaginative forgiveness* becomes more than a communication strategy used for conflict management or relationship maintenance by providing a transformative perspective that allows relational partners to view themselves and their relational worlds in a way that encourages and enables the co-creation of a shared, relational humanity. In this vein, we hold that . . .

Imaginative Forgiveness is a *relational process* whereby,

- **harmful conduct is acknowledged** by one or both partners;
- both partners **experience an emotional response** and **strive to make sense** of their new relational situation;
- the *offending partner imagines the harmed partner's perspective and responds with remorse, sincerity, and full apology*;
- the *harmed partner imagines the offending partner's perspective, empathizes, and responds with mercy* regarding the perceived transgression;
- partners experience a **transformation from destructive to constructive** cognitive, emotional, and/or behavioral responses;

- *understandings of self, partner, and relationship are reimagined and renegotiated*;
- and *possibly (re)enacted* when *safe conditions for reconciliation* are created or restored.

References

Arendt, H. (1958). *The human condition*. Chicago, IL: The University of Chicago Press.

Canary, D. J., & Stafford, L. (1992). Relational maintenance strategies and equity in marriage. *Communication Monographs, 59*, 243–267.

Chai, M., & Chai, W. (2001). *The girl from the purple mountain: Love, honor war, and one family's journey from China to America*. New York, NY: Thomas Dunne.

Cody, M. J., & McLaughlin, M. L. (1990). Interpersonal accounting. In H. Giles & W. P. Robinson (Eds.), *Handbook of language and social psychology* (pp. 227–255). Chichester, UK: Wiley.

Davis, J. L., Green, J. D., Reid, C. A., Moloney, J. M., & Burnette, J. (2015). Forgiveness and health in nonmarried dyadic relationships. In L. L. Toussaint, E. L. Worthington, & D. R. Williams (Eds.), *Forgiveness and health: Scientific evidence and theories relating to forgiveness and better health* (pp. 239–253). New York, NY: Springer.

Derrida, J. (2001). *On cosmopolitanism and forgiveness*. New York, NY: Routledge.

Enright, R. D. (2001). *Forgiveness is a choice: A step-by-step process for resolving anger and restoring hope*. Washington, DC: American Psychological Association.

Enright, R. D., Eastin, D. L., Golden, S., Sarinopoulos, I., & Freedman, S. (1992). Interpersonal forgiveness within the helping professions: An attempt to resolve differences of opinion. *Counseling and Values, 36*(2), 84–103.

Enright, R. D., & Fitzgibbons, R. P. (2000). *Helping clients forgive: An empirical guide for resolving anger and restoring hope* (1st ed.). Washington, DC: American Psychological Association.

Enright, R. D., Gassin, E. A., & Wu, C. R. (1992). Forgiveness: A developmental view. *Journal of Moral Education, 21*, 99–114.

Fincham, F. D. (2015). Forgiveness, family relationships and health. In L. L. Toussaint, E. L. Worthington, & D. R. Williams (Eds.), *Forgiveness and health: Scientific evidence and theories relating to forgiveness and better health* (pp. 255–270). New York, NY: Springer.

Foss, S. K., & Griffin, C. L. (1995). Beyond persuasion: A proposal for an invitational rhetoric. *Communication Monographs, 62*, 2–18.

Goman, C., & Kelley, D. (2016). Conceptualizing forgiveness in the face of historical trauma. In M. Casper & E. Wertheimer (Eds.), *Critical trauma studies: Understanding violence, conflict, and memory in everyday life*. New York: New York University Press.

Griswold, C. L. (2007). Plato and forgiveness. *Ancient Philosophy, 27*(2), 269–287. doi:10.5840/ancientphil20072723

Guerrero, L., & Cole, M. (2015). Moral standards, emotions, and communication associated with relational transgressions in dating relationships. In V. Waldron & D. Kelley (Eds.), *Moral talk across the lifespan: Creating good relationships* (pp. 155–182). New York, NY: Peter Lang.

Kearns, J. N., & Fincham, F. D. (2004). A prototype analysis of forgiveness. *Personality and Social Psychology Bulletin, 30*, 838–855.

Kelley, D. L. (1998). The communication of forgiveness. *Communication Studies, 49*, 255–271.

Kelley, D. L. (2017). *Just relationships: Living out social justice as mentor, family, friend, and lover*. New York, NY: Routledge.

Kelley, D. L., & Waldron, V. R. (2005). An investigation of forgiveness-seeking communication and relational outcomes. *Communication Quarterly, 53,* 339–358.

Kelley, D. L., Wolf, B. M., & Broberg, S. E. (2016, May). *Forgiveness communication and health. In The Oxford Research Encyclopedia of Communication.* New York, NY: Oxford University Press. doi:10.1093/acrefore/9780190228613.013.9

Kloeber, D. N. (2011). *Voicing conditional forgiveness.* Tempe: Arizona State University.

Kloeber, D. N., & Waldron, V. R. (2017). Expressing and suppressing conditional forgiveness in serious romantic relationships. In J. A. Samp (Ed.), *Communicating interpersonal conflict in close relationships: Contexts, challenges, and opportunities* (pp. 250–266). New York, NY: Routledge.

McCullough, M. E., Pargament, K. I., & Thoresen, C. E. (Eds.). (2000). *Forgiveness: Theory, research, and practice.* New York, NY: Guilford.

McNulty, J. K. (2011). The dark side of forgiveness: The tendency to forgive predicts continued psychological and physical aggression in marriage. *Personality & Social Psychology Bulletin, 37*(6), 770–783. doi:10.1177/0146167211407077

Merolla, A. J. (2008). Communicating forgiveness in friendships and dating relationships. *Communication Studies, 59*(2), 114–131. doi:10.1080/10510970802062428

Merolla, A. J. (2017). Forgiveness following conflict: What it is, why it happens, and how it's done. In J. A. Samp (Ed.), *Communicating interpersonal conflict in close relationships: Contexts, challenges, and opportunities* (pp. 227–249). New York, NY: Routledge.

Merolla, A. J., & Zhang, S. (2011). In the wake of transgression: Examining forgiveness communication in personal relationships. *Personal Relationships, 18,* 79–95.

Nhat Hanh, T. (2014). *No mud, no lotus: The art of transforming suffering.* Berkeley, CA: Parallax Press.

North, J. (1987). Wrongdoing and forgiveness. *Philosophy, 62,* 499–508.

North, J. (1998). The "ideal" of forgiveness: A philosopher's exploration. In R. D. Enright and J. North (Eds.), *Exploring forgiveness* (pp. 15–34). Madison, WI: The University of Wisconsin Press.

Nussbaum, M. C. (2016). *Anger and forgiveness: Resentment, generosity, justice.* New York, NY: Oxford University Press.

Prager, K. J. (1995). *The psychology of intimacy.* New York, NY: Guilford.

Ravsberg, F. (2016, April 7). Cuba: History, forgetfulness, resentment and forgiveness. *Havana Times.* Retrieved from https://havanatimes.org/?p=117966

Rye, M. S., Folck, C. D., Heim, T. A., Olszewski, B. T., & Traina, E. (2004). Forgiveness of an ex-spouse: How does it relate to mental health following a divorce? (author abstract). *Journal of Divorce and Remarriage, 41*(3–4), 31(21).

Rye, M. S., Pargament, K. I., Ali, M. A., Beck, G. L., Dorff, E. N., Hallisey, C., . . . Williams, J. G. (2000). Religious perspectives on forgiveness. In M. E. McCullough, K. I. Pargament, & C. E. Thoresen (Eds.), *Forgiveness: Theory, research, and practice* (pp. 17–40). New York, NY: The Guildford Press.

Schumann, K. (2012). Does love mean never having to say you're sorry? Associations between relationship satisfaction, perceived apology sincerity, and forgiveness. *Journal of Social and Personal Relationships, 29*(7), 997–1010. doi:10.1177/0265407512448277

Scobie, E. D., & Scobie, G. E. W. (1998). Damaging events: The perceived need for forgiveness. *Journal for the Theory of Social Behavior, 28,* 373–401.

The Dalai Lama. (1977/2003). In S. Wiesenthal (Ed.), *The sunflower: On the possibilities and limits of forgiveness* (p. 129). New York, NY: Schocken Books.

Toussaint, L. L., Worthington, Jr., E. L., & Williams, D. R. (2015). *Forgiveness and health: Scientific evidence and theories relating to forgiveness and better health.* New York, NY: Springer.

Tucker, J. R., Bitman, R. L., Wade, N. G., & Cornish, M. A. (2013). Defining forgiveness: Historical roots, contemporary research, and key considerations for health outcomes. In L. L. Toussaint, E. L. Worthington, Jr., & D. R. Williams (Eds.), *Forgiveness and health: Scientific evidence and theories relating forgiveness to better health* (pp. 13–28). Heidelberg, Germany: Springer.

Tutu, D. (1999). *No future without forgiveness.* New York, NY: Doubleday.

Volf, M. (2001). Forgiveness, reconciliation, and justice: A Christian contribution to a more peaceful social environment. In R. Helmick & R. L. Petersen (Eds.), *Forgiveness and reconciliation: Religion, public policy, and conflict transformation* (pp. 27–49). Philadelphia, PA: Templeton Foundation Press.

Vrij, A. (2006). Nonverbal communication and deception. In V. Manusov & M. L. Patterson (Eds.), *The Sage handbook of nonverbal communication* (pp. 341–360). Thousand Oaks, CA: Sage. Retrieved from http://dx.doi.org.ezproxy1.lib.asu.edu/10.4135/9781412 976152.n18

Waldron, V. R., & Kelley, D. (2005). Forgiveness as a response to relational transgression. *Journal of Social and Personal Relationships, 22*, 723–742.

Waldron, V. R., & Kelley, D. L. (2008). *Communicating forgiveness.* Thousand Oaks, CA: Sage.

Wiesenthal, S. (2008). *The sunflower: On the possibilities and limits of forgiveness.* New York, NY: Schocken Books.

Worthington, E. L., Jr. (2005). *Handbook of forgiveness.* New York, NY: Routledge.

Worthington, E. L., Jr. (2006). *Forgiveness and reconciliation: Theory and application.* New York, NY: Routledge.

7

RECONCILIATION

Imagining a New Future

When we arrived at John and Mary's home in an active retirement community in the Phoenix metropolitan area, Mary was quick to confess that she and John were not married . . . they had been married, and were currently living together, but had not remarried. Our study was specifically directed at long-term married couples. Our screener explicitly asked whether couples met the minimum criteria to be in the study, namely – "Have you been married at least 30 years?" Well, there we were, so we might as well go through with this and see what we could learn. Mary told much of the story, while John sat quietly, adding in his "two cents" every now and then. It turned out that after John's short affair, Mary and John divorced, but often saw one another at events involving their children. The reality was that they still loved each other, but Mary could not go back into a relationship like they had before – "I will never fall back into that trap, again!" John truly loved and missed Mary, and even though she wouldn't remarry him, he did convince her to try living together. Their, now adult, children provided a loving warning, "Mom, you know we love Dad, but we hope you know what you are doing." After two years of cohabitating, John still wants to get married, but Mary likes life too much to change things, at least for the time being – John actually cooks and does laundry this time around! Mary clearly loves to have fun with her former husband and, now, current lover, even joking with him early in the interview, "He is still writing me $1000 alimony checks each month!"

★

John and Mary's relational journey provides an intriguing example of the complexities of reconciliation – emotional healing, reestablished commitment, rebuilt trust, all interacting in ways that enable this regenerated couple the ability to (re)imagine and (re)create a positive, just and loving future together. Their reimagined relationship is certainly not a "return to normal" or anything either of them could have predicted. To unpack the complex nature of reconciliation, in this chapter we overview various social science perspectives and offer a communication-based model of reconciliation, ultimately addressing the imaginative art of reconciliation.

What Does It Mean to Reconcile?

Reconciliation seems simple enough at first glance. One or both relationship partners violate a relationship expectation, norm, rule, or moral ethic. The violation hurts at least one relational partner and damages the relationship. The partners find a way to repair the relationship. Simple. Yet, what actually constitutes "repair", and how this is accomplished, can baffle the most talented relationship partners. Our own research has shown that reconciliation may manifest as strengthened or weakened relationships, a returning to normal, or even a change in relationship type (e.g., dating to friendship; Kelley, 1998).

Words and phrases commonly associated with reconciliation, such as *repair*, *return to normal*, and *restore*, contribute to the confusion. These words conjure little in terms of relational imagination. They are reminiscent of having one's car fixed ("Runs like new!"). Yet, a more robust picture emerges from reconciliation stories. Couples who survive relationship transgressions, like Mary and John at the chapter's opening, frequently report a strengthening of the relationship. Even more than reaffirming the same old structure, relational partners are often pushed, because of their relationship trauma, to reinvent themselves. Doug's story regarding counseling with his wife illustrates this point. They didn't simply rebuild their emotional connection, they learned to emotionally connect in ways they hadn't experienced before. Through dialogue and recognition of patterns that were no longer beneficial for the relationship, they began to experience shifts in perspective and emotion, leading to hope and the reimagination and re-creation of their marriage. As we discuss in *Chapter 2*, relationship reimagination, as a means of reconciliation, is a process that recognizes existing and past patterns, uses dialogue to create change in perspective, emotional experience, and behavioral sequences, and engenders hope and the eventual re-creation of a benevolent and just relational future.

How We Reconcile

Social scientists have narrowed the constituent elements of reconciliation to a few central components. Rusbult, Hannon, Stocker, and Finkel (2005), operating from an interdependence theory perspective, hold that reconciliation is, "the successful resumption of pretransgression relationship status" (p. 199) and that reconciliation is dependent on restoring commitment and trust through the significant mutual investment of both parties. *Commitment* is defined as, "the extent to which each partner intends to persist in the relationship, feels psychologically attached to it, and exhibits long-term orientation toward it" (p. 187), while *trust* is identified as, "the strength of each partner's conviction that the other can be counted on to behave in a benevolent manner" (p. 187). Practically speaking, commitment is the assurance that one is not going to just walk away from the relationship. There is an allegiance, a willingness to work through the hard times. Trust is the degree to which one believes the other person will choose to act kindly, compassionately, with consideration for the other, perhaps even accommodating, sacrificing for, and affirming the partner. Thus, in order to effect lasting repair, both partners must make mutual prosocial investments in the relationship. For example, an offended party may act with good will, setting aside blame and accusation in the hopes of starting anew and working together, while the offender simultaneously decides to take responsibility for the transgression, seeking to make amends and jointly change unwanted patterns of behavior.

Worthington (2006) states that, "Reconciliation is restoring trust" (p. 197), and makes trust a key element of his clinical model, *Forgiveness and Reconciliation through Experiencing Empathy* (FREE; Worthington, 2006; Worthington & Drinkard, 2000). FREE uses a bridge metaphor to help clients imagine and work toward reconciliation during therapy. Plank 1 in the bridge is *Decision: Should I Discuss Transgressions?* This first step focuses on decisions to reconcile, possibly talk about transgressions, and if appropriate explore how and when to reconcile. Plank 2, *Discussion: How Do People Talk About Transgressions?*, emphasizes therapeutic goals (including an emphasis on repairing the emotional bond), and exercises for discussing transgressions that include such elements as establishing ground rules, listening, and teaching partners how to make useful reproaches, give and respond to confession, and possibly forgive. Plank 3, *Detoxification of Relationships: How Do We Repair the Damage?*, highlights stopping and changing negative behaviors, cognitions, and situations. *Devotion: How Can We Put the Positive Back Into the Relationship and Rebuild Trust?*, is the final plank that emphasizes valuing one's partner through positive interaction, and rebuilding trust and devotion.

In a model designed to help couples negotiate the often treacherous relational territory that exists after an extramarital affair, Gordon and Baucom (2003) and Gordon, Baucom, and Snyder (2000) describe a three-stage process that may facilitate reconciliation. Stage I, *Impact*, is characterized by feelings of uncertainty, violated trust, and increased risk. Often with the help of a therapist, during this stage the wounded partner places boundaries on interactions with the offender, practices self-care, uses time-out and venting strategies, copes with flashbacks, and discusses the impact of the transgression with the offender (Gordon & Baucom, 1999). The second phase, *Meaning*, is characterized by communication behavior intended to reduce uncertainty and increase mutual understanding. A goal is to restore losses of control and security while determining whether the relationship can be safely reconciled. In the third stage, *Recovery* or *Moving on*, the understanding that has been developed at the *meaning* stage leads to a "non-distorted view" (Gordon & Baucom, 2003, p. 182) and less intense negative emotion. The offended party may recognize that forgiveness is preferable to revenge because the latter will not "rebalance" the relationship. During this stage the pair may negotiate forgiveness and work through problematic issues that could affect their reconciliation. For these authors, the task of forgiveness is embedded within a larger process of potential reconciliation.

Reconciliation as Communication

At the heart of reconciliation are communicative processes that cultivate adaptive emotional expressions and cognitive and behavioral restructuring of the relationship. Our previous work (Kelley, 1998; Kelley & Waldron, 2005; Waldron & Kelley, 2005, 2008) demonstrates that reconciliation actually takes a variety of forms and is influenced by various forgiveness-granting and -seeking strategies. For instance, strengthening of relationships has been associated with extending forgiveness through explicitly saying "I forgive you" (or the equivalent), discussion, and nonverbal assurance (the three of these create an unequivocal and sincere response). Likewise, seeking forgiveness through explicit acknowledgment (e.g., apology) and nonverbal assurance (e.g., sincerity) has been positively associated with post-transgression change in relationship quality and intimacy. Using compensation to seek forgiveness has also been associated with positive post-transgression change in intimacy, though it wasn't used frequently by the couples we studied. Interestingly, conditional forgiveness is regularly associated with a weakening of the relationship. Consistent with these findings, Merolla (2017) states that, "conditional forgiveness indeed presents a series of conundrums for researches to make sense of" (p. 238). Dayna (Kloeber, 2011; Kloeber & Waldron, 2017) has examined the practice in detail, finding that conditional forgiveness is often used as a protective device (e.g., setting boundaries/conditions) providing the harmed party with assurance that the harmful act will not be repeated.

Communicating to Reconcile

In an effort to emphasize communicative aspects of relationship restoration, Kelley (2012a) offers a four-stage perspective by drawing parallels between Waldron and Kelley's (2008) *Communication Tasks of Forgiveness* (see *Chapter 5*) and Gordon et al.'s (2000) and Gordon and Baucom's (2003) three-stage approach to forgiveness (discussed previously and designed for couples who have experienced infidelity). The four stages emphasize communication tasks and begin with *managing the impact*, a focusing on the restoration of individual well-being by confronting a transgression and managing emotion. Second, *making sense of one's self, partner, and relationship* begins the reestablishment of the moral code of the relationship through discussion, explanation, listening, and engaging in perspective-taking. Third, *engaging forgiveness* restores well-being and the relationship moral order through apology, nonverbal assurance, sensitivity, empathy, and forgiveness seeking and granting. Finally, *negotiating reconciliation* is a process of relationship restoration through the renegotiation of rules and values, and the co-creation of new relationship behavioral patterns and moral codes.

Communicatively Charged Reconciliation

Kelley (2017) also offers a more comprehensive communication-based approach to reconciliation, based on work by Worthington and Drinkard (2000) and Worthington (2006). This effort reformulates their six planks into six charges, or exhortations, with specific focus on key aspects of communication. Here, we expand on this approach. *Communicatively Charged Reconciliation (CCR)* emphasizes six communication charges (goals/exhortations), any of which may occur in tandem, and in any order, as partners move toward reconciliation (Box 7.1). While it makes sense that certain charges may be initiated or become more prominent at various times in the process, each charge is to be processed over time as they emerge and reemerge.

BOX 7.1 COMMUNICATIVELY CHARGED RECONCILIATION (CCR)*

The following represent six communication charges, or goals, that work in tandem with one another during the reconciliation process.

Charge 1: Commit to Explore Reconciliation.
Charge 2: Rehumanize Your Partner.
Charge 3: Choose to Heal your Emotional Pain.
Charge 4: Rebuild Broken Trust.
Charge 5: Imaginatively Create New, Positive Patterns.
Charge 6: Commit to Love and Personal Advocacy.

*Based on work by Worthington and Drinkard (2000; Worthington, 2006) and Kelley (2017).

Charge 1: Commit to Explore Reconciliation

The first charge is to *commit to explore reconciliation*. It is tempting to think the charge to explore and commit is the beginning of the reconciliation process, but commonly individuals begin exploring reconciliation without a full commitment to the process. They are "testing the waters", so to speak, to determine whether or not it is emotionally and psychologically safe, and worth the energy, to pursue the process (Kloeber, 2011). Useful when engaging this charge is dialogue with one's partner or safe individuals in one's social network.

As partners commit to explore reconciliation, it can be helpful for each individual to examine the nature of their own commitment to reconciliation. For example, motivation may be rooted externally in cultural or familial standards ("We don't believe in divorce"), or internally in personal values ("I am not a quitter") or relationship experience ("I still love her", "We've put too much into this relationship to let it die, now"). Of course, motivations to reconcile exist on a continuum of healthy (honest curiosity as to whether the relationship can be restored positively) to unhealthy (e.g., codependent attachment), and, as such, communication within one's social support network can be critical as one pursues reconciliation. Trusted friends and wise counselors may help surface unacknowledged motives and potential red flags.

Initially, the charge *commit to explore* may appear more cognitive than communicative, but maintaining commitment is an essential part of the communication process because as partners work out their reconciliation they will be misunderstood, as well as understood; hurt, as well as healed; frustrated, as well as celebrated. Reconciliation, at its best, is a messy process that unfolds over time and, as such, partners must renew their commitment throughout the process.

Charge 2: Rehumanize Your Partner

Clearly, dehumanizing works against our ability to engage in productive rehabilitation of damaged relationships as it creates emotional damage and hopelessness. When individuals experience relationship trauma or disappointment, they often act in ways that dehumanize the offending partner. Dehumanizing responses may be intended to restore justice (Kelley, 2017) or, as Worthington and Drinkard (2000) state, "partners who have been harmed by each other usually harden their defenses to minimize additional injury" (p. 96). Dehumanization comes in many forms, but it often typecasts offenders, portraying them as unredeemable and unworthy of consideration ("You are just like your father. You'll never change!") (Kelley, 2017). Unfortunately, this process can "legitimize" harsh, inhumane treatment of others, such as name calling or making painful accusations.

Worthington and Drinkard (2000) refer to this part of the process as "softening", and consider it one of the most challenging and important aspects of reconciliation. Rehumanizing one's partner, through softening one's perceptions and behaviors, is most clearly seen in the active engagement of empathy. As we discussed in *Chapter 5*, empathy is a perception-based sense-making process that enables understanding through imagination of the other's thoughts and emotional experience (Davis, 1983; Kelley, 2017).

The empathy process is facilitated through *genuine dialogue* (Buber, 1967) by creating a "living mutual relation" between partners (p. 113). Baxter and Montgomery (1996) identify four dialogic principles that we believe, when adopted by relationship partners, are useful to achieving empathy (Box 7.2). The first principle, *competent interaction reifies contradiction*, encourages partners to embrace the inconsistencies and ambivalences that emerge in any complex relationship. Second, *competent interaction reifies respect for multivocality*, emphasizing respect for others' perspectives, and may produce positive results in terms of process (feeling understood by one another) and outcome (creating better decisions). Third, *competent interaction reifies fluid dialogue* places emphasis on determining what actions or perspectives may limit dialogue and, as such, limit empathy and the overall quality of the interaction. Here, partners note how their own aggressive or avoidant responses may block empathy and productive dialogue. Finally, *competent interaction reifies creativity* highlights the imaginative properties of empathy itself, by suggesting that proactive, imaginative communication characterizes relationship excellence.

BOX 7.2 APPLICATION OF BAXTER AND MONTGOMERY'S FOUR DIALOGIC PRINCIPLES*

- **Embracing Contradiction**: What can you learn from your partner's perspective, even if you disagree with him or her?
- **Respecting Voices Other than One's Own**: Think of an issue where you and your partner hold differing opinions: How can you show respect for your partner's thinking and work together to create a joint decision regarding this issue?
- **Maintaining Ongoing Conversation**: Make an assessment of what types of behaviors might be shutting down open dialogue in your relationship.
- **Being Creative**: How are you and your partner responding creatively to keep your relationship moving forward in ways that benefit you both? Are there areas of your relationship that could use more creativity?

*Borrowed from Kelley (2017, pp. 24–25)

Charge 3: Choose to Heal Your Emotional pain

The third reconciliation charge is *choose to heal your emotional pain*. One's emotional pain, if not healed or at least in the process of being healed, will inevitably become a barrier to reconciliation efforts. In this regard, forgiveness plays a unique role in the full reconciliation process because forgiveness is uniquely positioned to heal negative emotional experience. Worthington (2006) promotes the notion that forgiveness is, in part, "replacing negative, unforgiving stressful emotions with positive, other-oriented emotions" (Worthington, 2006, p. 17).

A focus on constructive emotion-based experience is especially relevant to the reconciliation of partners in close relationships because emotional connection is central to the development of loving partnerships. Kelley (2012b) conceptualizes emotional bonding as an essential element of love which, along with commitment and other-centeredness, creates a safe place for intimacy to emerge. Congruently, Emotionally Focused Therapy (EFT) for couples, as the name suggests, is a counseling approach that focuses on rebuilding lost or damaged emotional connection between partners. Proponents claim high success rates in moving damaged relationships to recovery through reestablishing emotional reconnection.

As Doug has referenced previously, part of the relational healing between his wife and himself came through working with an EFT counselor. Doug reports that he disliked going to sessions because the emotion focus was something he couldn't control as readily as more cognitively based approaches. Rather than solving their relational problems ("If she would just do X, we would be fine"), they learned to be vulnerably present with one another. For example, at one point when Doug was sharing, the therapist asked him to turn toward Ann. As Doug looked and saw tears in Ann's eyes, the therapist asked what he was feeling. As he shared his own sadness at having hurt her, there was a deeper sense of emotional connection between the two of them. Being authentically present became the key to healing past hurts and moving forward toward a healthy, trusting, reimagined future.

Charge 4: Rebuild Broken Trust

Ann and Doug's story also highlights the fourth communicatively based charge that facilitates reconciliation – *rebuild broken trust*. Mutual confidence in one another can only be repaired over time as partners reestablish emotional connection, engage in honest dialogue, and exhibit predictable patterns of behavior. Attempts to restore trust through means such as simple apologies may be perceived as too easy and unrealistic ("I promise, that will never happen again").

However, restoring confidence in one another is tricky relational territory. As Worthington and Drinkard (2000) suggest, "it is critical to persuade partners that failures in trustworthiness are not only unsurprising but are, in fact, to be expected" (p. 98). Often, rebuilding trust does not progress in a linear manner (e.g., a straight line of growth from transgression to "perfect" behavior). This may create an obstacle to restoration as partners experience a sense of vulnerability while they watch and hope for behavioral change. Essentially, we trust those whom we think are safe for us, whom we believe would not intentionally or carelessly (even if unintentional) harm us. Once that belief is broken, and we are hurt by the person we trusted, it can be a significant risk to consider reengaging the partner and the relationship. This substantial risk may result in attempts to control or monitor the transition process in ways that may or may not be constructive, such as implementing conditional forgiveness (Kloeber & Waldron, 2017; Waldron & Kelley, 2008). Essential is establishing a space to safely (re)experience emotional vulnerability and trust with one another.

Charge 5: Imaginatively Create New, Positive Patterns

The process of engendering safe, trustworthy ways of relating represents the fifth communicatively based reconciliation charge – *imaginatively creating new, positive patterns* in the relationship. One approach to changing patterns for the "good" is found in Negotiated Morality Theory (NMT; Waldron & Kelley, 2008). NMT suggests that rebuilding trusting, intimate, just relationships can be accomplished through the successful renegotiation of relationship values during the forgiveness process. This might result in renewed commitments to such core relational values as mutual respect or sexual fidelity. Indeed, the co-creation of a new relationship ethic is a central and necessary task when rebuilding a relationship after couples experience betrayal (Gordon & Baucom 2003; Gordon et al., 2000; Kelley, 2012b). Having productive dialogue, for many couples, may itself be a significant achievement.

Part of creating space for productive dialogue is identifying and changing pre-existing dysfunctional communication patterns. Worthington and Drinkard (2000) highlight Gottman's *Cascade Model of Marital Dissolution* (1994) in an effort to reverse the cascade of negative behavior that is frequently so destructive in long-term relationships. The *Cascade Model*, or *The Four Horsemen of the Apocalypse*, has been well supported by therapeutic-based research (Olson & Donahey, 2018), and proposes that dissatisfied couples experience a cascade of negative behavior beginning with *criticism* and *defensiveness* that, if not disrupted, eventually results in feelings and expressions of *contempt* and *stonewalling* (psychological and emotional withdrawal). These latter responses are of greater concern as they indicate emotional distancing between relational partners has become more prominent, requiring the emotional connection between partners to be reestablished if the pair hopes for a renewed future together.

Charge 6: Commit to Love and Personal Advocacy

The final charge for reconciling relational partners is *commit to love and personal advocacy*. Whereas charges three and five highlight the importance of rebuilding emotional connection (an aspect consistently connected to the idea of love; Fredrickson, 2013; Kelley, 2012b), the emphasis in this charge is on cognitive, decisional aspects of love (Kelley, 2012b; Sternberg, 1986, 1997) that ensure the intent to continue work on what may be a long, at times trying, process. In this light, North (1987) views forgiveness as a "willed change of heart" characterized by "compassion and affection" (p. 506). Enright, Eastin, Golden, Sarinopoulos, and Freedman (1992) go so far as to claim forgiveness imparts love toward the other person, a response engendered by the choice to love.

Another key aspect of love, as it relates to reconciliation, is *other-centeredness*. Kelley (2012b) argues that deep emotional connection (as opposed to transient feelings) and commitment may result in healthy self-sacrifice (Stanley, Whitton, Sadberry, Clements, & Markman, 2006). Together these three elements create a safe place for relational partners to be vulnerable. In this way, love actually becomes a form of advocacy, *"creating a safe space where if something good can happen, it will"* (Kelley, 2017). That is, full love creates a space where each partner, feeling valued (Worthington & Drinkard, 2000), can safely find and express his or her own voice and, thus, together co-create a just future.

We want to again emphasize that these six communicative charges for reconciliation may occur in any order and often take place concurrently. For example, the processes of rehumanizing one's partner and rebuilding trust will likely be reciprocal – the more you become "human" to me, the more I trust you; and, the more I trust you, the more I can see you as fully human – and may work in tandem with creating new positive patterns as we advocate for one another and our future relationship.

Unique Communicative Considerations

Two uniquely communicative processes shape the character of many reconciliation attempts – conditional forgiveness/reconciliation and full apology. Although we have referenced these concepts in previous chapters, here we take a closer look due to their importance during reconciliation, and because they often present substantial communication challenges.

Conditional Forgiveness/Reconciliation and Setting Boundaries

Conditional forgiveness is a type of forgiveness-granting that places stipulations on the offender (Kelley, 1998; Waldron & Kelley, 2008; see *Chapter 6*). For example, I'll forgive you for getting a DUI (driving under the influence), as long as you'll start attending AA meetings (Kloeber, 2011). This is a commonly used forgiveness strategy, especially in long-term, committed relationships (Guerrero & Bachmann, 2010; Kloeber, 2011; Merolla & Zhang, 2011; Waldron & Kelley, 2008), and it is more often used when transgressions are perceived as severe (Merolla & Zhang, 2011; Waldron & Kelley, 2005), which may include events such as relational neglect, disrespect, infidelity, disregard, betrayal, and even abuse. People who use conditional forgiveness in serious romantic relationships do so for a variety of reasons that include (a) to weigh their relational history (i.e., investment, relational satisfaction, repeated offenses), (b) to restore or enact relational moral standards, (c) to clarify personal needs or expectations, (d) to protect themselves or their partners, (e) to enact justice or exert control, (f) to provide a best alternative to unconditional or genuine forgiveness, or (g) because they hope for an improved future (Kloeber & Waldron, 2017).

Our choice to discuss conditional forgiveness in this chapter on reconciliation highlights messy conceptual dilemmas associated with the concept. Quite a few years ago at a conference, a veteran scholar, harkening to theological understandings of forgiveness, rhetorically asked, "You do know there is no such thing as conditional forgiveness?" A few years later, another scholar posed an equally evocative question: "Is there any other kind of forgiveness?" Her point was a good one: When hoping to remain in the relationship, do we ever truly forgive unconditionally? Or do we instead imagine and hope for a better future when we forgive? In essence, do people actually conditionally forgive or do they, actually, conditionally reconcile? Kloeber's (2011) study of serious romantic partners who reported the use of conditional forgiveness discovered an overarching dialectical tension in participants' reports: reconcilable–irreconcilable. Further, while a few participants reported conditionally forgiving without regard to reconciling, most were also actively negotiating the boundaries of their reconciliation. Kloeber's analysis also found that serious romantic partners who grant conditional forgiveness were weighing a plethora of complex factors, including how the transgression affected both individual and couple identity, how emotionally and physically safe they felt in the current state of their relationship, to what degree they believed trust could be rebuilt, and how much to verbally express or suppress the relational conditions, or boundaries, they deemed necessary.

Interestingly, conditional forgiveness has been consistently associated with reduced relational satisfaction, above and beyond the effects of transgression severity (Merolla & Zhang, 2011; Waldron & Kelley, 2005). Relational outcomes are also associated with whether conditions are expressed or suppressed (Kloeber, 2011; Kloeber & Waldron, 2017). Explicitly expressed conditions are associated with relational strengthening in serious romantic relationships, and suppressed conditions associated with relational weakening (Kloeber & Waldron, 2017). The reasons for these effects are still unclear, but scholars have speculated that setting conditions, especially when suppressed, may create power imbalances that inhibit a reconciliation based on equality. Whereas explicit boundary setting may involve dialogue when boundaries are being set, maintaining suppressed conditions may be viewed as continued attempts to exert control and monitor the partner's behavior (Merolla & Zhang, 2011; Merolla, Zhang, & Sun, 2013; Waldron & Kelley, 2005, 2008). For example, consider two possible scenarios between Bianca and Katie in Box 7.3.

It is important to note, here, that while this book focuses on *reimagining our relationships,* not all relationships should be reconciled. A handful of the respondents

BOX 7.3 EXPLICIT CONDITIONAL FORGIVENESS

Scenario One

Bianca: I need to be free to check your phone history until we rebuild trust.

Katie: That seems crazy. I can just delete texts and calls.

Bianca: I know, but until we've worked at this awhile, I just need more assurance.

Katie: Okay, I guess I can understand that.

Scenario Two

Katie: When are you going to quit picking up my phone to check the history?! I know you do it when I'm not in the room.

Bianca: Look, you're the one who had the affair. You are going to have to live with the consequences until you prove to me I can trust you.

Katie: Then maybe we should quit, now. I'm never going to be "perfect" enough for you!

in Kloeber's (2011) study reported they conditionally forgave partners for extreme physical abuse. One in particular said her boyfriend held her down and choked her. Another said her husband chased her down the hallway with a knife and she locked herself in the bathroom overnight. Most of the forgiveness stories we have collected over the past 20 years are not nearly this dramatic or toxic, but we are cognizant that conditional forgiveness may respond to a darker side of relationships (Kloeber & Waldron, 2017). If these badly damaged bonds are to be reimagined, assistance from mental health professionals will almost certainly be required.

Full Apology

A common question from potential forgivers is, "Does the offender need to apologize before I forgive her?" Indeed, as we just discussed, receiving a sincere apology could be a condition of forgiveness or reconciliation. The complex issue of when apology is necessary typically involves questions of justice and safety. In essence, the humility necessary to offer a sincere apology helps to restore a sense of equity in the relationship, and an apology that demonstrates true understanding, remorse, and a commitment to change future behavior helps the offended party feel safe, and that the hurtful behavior is less likely occur again.

Apology is particularly relevant to the reconciliation process because full apologies constitute many of the necessary pieces of healthy reuniting (Kelley, 2017; Waldron & Kelley, 2008). As discussed throughout this chapter, reconciliation involves the reestablishment of trust and commitment in the relationship, and both facilitate and require emotional vulnerability from each partner. In this light, consider Lazare's (2005) discussion of apology:

> Two parties must participate in an interaction at high risk of producing discomfort: The offender, in a position of a supplicant who exposes weakness and risks rejection or retaliation; and the offended party, who may be uncomfortable with the other person's embarrassment or may be reluctant to relinquish a treasured grudge or even admit being hurt. Thus, the entire process of offering, negotiating, or accepting an apology can be emotionally demanding for both parties.
>
> (p. 229)

Sincerity has been often associated with effective apology. Ebesu Hubbard, Hendrickson, Fehrenbach, and Sur's (2013) examination of the role of apology, timing, and sincerity on relational outcomes found that sincerity was positively associated with communication satisfaction and less hard emotions, such as anger. Similarly, Schumann (2012) reported that highly satisfied individuals were more forgiving after a partner apologized because they perceived the apology as sincere, showing remorse. Similarly, Waldron and Kelley (2008) found apology to be associated with expression of remorse, and that nonverbal assurance was commonly used when explicitly seeking forgiveness.

An interesting study using magnetic resonance imagining (iMRI) measured variance in brain activation by type of apology, in particular focusing on the effect of costly apologies, which included reparation or intent to make up for the transgression, and which likely demonstrated sincerity. Ohtsubo et al. (2018) examined differences in the theory-of-mind (TofM) network between costly apology (e.g., apology with reparation), non-costly apology (e.g., a simple "I'm sorry" with short explanation/excuse), and no apology. The TofM (bilateral temporoparietal junction, precuneus, and medial prefrontal cortex) is associated with social and communicative intention, and hypothesized to be activated by conciliatory behavior. To potentially activate TofM, researchers asked participants to read scenarios describing a friend having committed a mild interpersonal transgression (e.g., failed to invite you to a get-together with friends; posted a secret you meant to keep private) and then scenarios wherein the offender offered a costly apology, non-costly apology (e.g., a simple "I'm sorry"), or no apology. Results indicated more activation of the TofM for costly apologies, as compared to non-costly apologies and non-apologies. Underscoring our previous discussion, Ohtsubo et al. (2018) suggest that, "merely saying sorry can fail to convey a sincere intention to restore an endangered relationship. In such cases, conciliatory signals must be costly. The cost of an apology makes transparent the transgressor's benign, non-exploitative intent" (p. 254), although it should be noted that Ohtsubo et al.'s (2018) findings do not take into account potential effects of relationship quality (see Schumann, 2012).

Lazare's (2005) list of reasons that apology heals rounds out our discussion of the role of apology when reconciling. Lazare believes that apologies fulfill one or more of the following psychological needs of the offended party, paving the way for reconciliation: Restoration of self-respect and dignity, assurance of shared values between the partners, assurance that the offense was not the fault of the offended party, assurance of psychological and physical safety in the relationship, seeing the offender suffer (i.e., reestablishing justice in the relationship and demonstrating sincerity on the part of the offender), reparation for harm caused, and having meaningful dialogues with the offender (i.e., creating space for the offended party to voice her or his experience and hear from the offender). Note that one or more of these will be most important to each relational partner and, as such, effective apologies will vary by relationship. Central to the process, however, is establishing personal well-being, mutuality between partners, safety, and justice. Meaningful dialogue, while not guaranteeing successful reconciliation, potentially forecasts key aspects of a healthy future relationship.

A Couple of Final Imaginings

Often, when we conduct community workshops on forgiveness and reconciliation (see *Chapter 8*), people ask how to know if they should reengage the person who hurt them. It can be difficult to imagine the myriad possible outcomes of beginning the reconciliation process.

Here, we offer a few simple guidelines for determining readiness to reconcile. First, establish whether the relational partner and situation is physically and psychologically safe. To begin forgiveness and/or reconciliation with an offender when she is not a safe person with whom to interact may lead to being re-victimized – the offended party finding herself back in a position where she is abused or manipulated. Charge 5 of *CCR* emphasizes the replacement of old, destructive patterns with new, positive patterns. Stepping into an unsafe environment can short-circuit this process such that partners are re-immersed in negative, hurtful interactions, all too reminiscent of their past. Second, if the person and situation is safe, both parties should do a motivation check. That is, each partner should ask: Why am I pursuing or open to this relationship that has been so hurtful? As we have stated throughout the book, working through relationship trauma can bring partners to deep levels of connection and vulnerability that strengthen and enrich the relationship. However, when motivations are unhealthy, we can find ourselves embroiled in controlling or codependent relationships. Finally, both parties should assess their own social support networks. Reconciliation processes rarely proceed smoothly and, as such, it is critical to have a support network in place when the process is not moving along as one hoped. Friends, family, and trusted mentors or counselors are important sources of encouragement and emotional support, but also often see the things we are unable to see about ourselves and our relationships.

Imagination clearly plays a central role when reconciling. Nothing ever goes back to exactly the way it was. It is necessary to use imagination constructively to engage the past, enable empathy and understanding, and co-create a positive future. In this chapter, we have emphasized six communicative charges that facilitate reconciliation. Each charge engages our personal and joint imaginations, helping partners negotiate a moral process whereby each person, and their shared relationship, experiences transformation and hope for the future.

References

Baxter, L. A., & Montgomery, B. M. (1996). *Relating: Dialogues and dialectics.* New York, NY: Guilford.

Buber, M. (1967). Between man and man: The realms. In F. W. Matson & A. Montagu (Eds.), *The human dialogue: Perspectives on communication* (pp. 113–117). New York, NY: The Free Press.

Davis, M. H. (1983). Measuring individual differences in empathy: Evidence for a multidimensional approach. *Journal of Personality and Social Psychology, 44*, 113–126.

Ebesu Hubbard, A. S., Hendrickson, B., Fehrenbach, K. S., & Sur, J. (2013). Effects of timing and sincerity of an apology on satisfaction and changes in negative feelings during conflicts. *Western Journal of Communication, 77*(3), 305–322.

Enright, R. D., Eastin, D. L., Golden, S., Sarinopoulos, I., & Freedman, S. (1992). Interpersonal forgiveness within the helping professions: An attempt to resolve differences of opinion. *Counseling and Values, 36*(2), 84–103.

Fredrickson, B. (2013). *Love 2.0: How our supreme emotion affects everything we feel, think, do, and become.* New York, NY: Hudson Street Press.

Gordon, K. C., & Baucom, D. H. (1999). A multitheoretical intervention for promoting recovery from extramarital affairs. *Clinical Psychology: Science and Practice, 6*, 382–399.

Gordon, K. C., & Baucom, D. H. (2003). Forgiveness and marriage: Preliminary support for a measure based on a model of recovery from a marital betrayal. *American Journal of Family Therapy, 31*, 179–199.

Gordon, K. C., Baucom, D. H., & Snyder, D. K. (2000). The use of forgiveness in marital therapy. In M. C. McCullough, K. I. Pargament, & C. E. Thoresen (Eds.), *Forgiveness: Theory, research, and practice* (pp. 203–227). New York, NY: Guilford.

Gottman, J. M. (1994). *What predicts divorce? The relationship between marital processes and marital outcomes.* Hillsdale, NJ: Lawrence Erlbaum.

Guerrero, L. K., & Bachman, G. F. (2010). Forgiveness and forgiving communication in dating relationships: An expectancy–investment explanation. *Journal of Social and Personal Relationships, 27*, 801–823.

Kelley, D. L. (1998). The communication of forgiveness. *Communication Studies, 49*, 255–271.

Kelley, D. L. (2012a). Forgiveness as restoration: The search for well-being, reconciliation, and relational justice. In T. J. Socha & M. J. Pitts (Eds.), *The positive side of interpersonal communication* (pp. 193–210). New York, NY: Peter Lang.

Kelley, D. L. (2012b). *Marital communication.* Cambridge, UK: Polity Press.

Kelley, D. L. (2017). *Just relationships: Living out social justice as mentor, family, friend, and lover.* New York, NY: Routledge.

Kelley, D. L., & Waldron, V. R. (2005). An investigation of forgiveness-seeking communication and relational outcomes. *Communication Quarterly, 53*, 339–358.

Kloeber, D. N. (2011). *Voicing conditional forgiveness.* Tempe: Arizona State University.

Kloeber, D. N., & Waldron, V. R. (2017). Expressing and suppressing conditional forgiveness in serious romantic relationships. In J. A. Samp (Ed.), *Communicating interpersonal conflict in close relationships: Contexts, challenges, and opportunities* (pp. 250–266). New York, NY: Routledge.

Lazare, A. (2005). *On apology.* New York, NY: Oxford University Press.

Merolla, A. J. (2017). Forgiveness following conflict: What it is, why it happens, and how it's done. In J. A. Samp (Ed.), *Communicating interpersonal conflict in close relationships: Contexts, challenges, and opportunities* (pp. 227–249). New York, NY: Routledge.

Merolla, A. J., & Zhang, S. (2011). In the wake of transgression: Examining forgiveness communication in personal relationships. *Personal Relationships, 18*, 79–95. doi:10.1111/j.1475–6811.2010.01323.x

Merolla, A. J., Zhang, S., & Sun, S. (2013). Forgiveness in the United States and China. *Communication Research, 40*(5), 595–622. doi:10.1177/0093650212446960

North, J. (1987). Wrongdoing and forgiveness. *Philosophy, 62*, 499–508.

Ohtsubo, Y., Matsunaga, M., Tanaka, H., Suzuki, K., Kobayashi, F., Shibata, E., . . . Ohira, H. (2018). Costly apologies communicate conciliatory intention: An fMRI study on forgiveness in response to costly apologies. *Evolution and Human Behavior, 39*(2), 249–256. doi:10.1016/j.evolhumbehav.2018.01.004

Olson, L. N., & Donahey, A. (2018). Four horsemen of the apocalypse: A framework for understanding family conflict. In D. O. Braithwaite, E. A. Suter, & K. Floyd (Eds.), *Engaging theories in family communication: Multiple perspectives* (2nd ed., pp. 154–163). New York, NY: Taylor & Francis.

Rusbult, C. E., Hannon, P. A., Stocker, S. L., & Finkel, E. J. (2005). Forgiveness and relational repair. In E. L. Worthington, Jr. (Ed.), *Handbook of forgiveness* (pp. 185–205). New York, NY: Routledge.

Schumann, K. (2012). Does love mean never having to say you're sorry? Associations between relationship satisfaction, perceived apology sincerity, and forgiveness. *Journal of Social and Personal Relationships, 29*(7), 997–1010. doi:10.1177/0265407512448277

Stanley, S. M., Whitton, S. W., Sadberry, S. L., Clements, M. L., & Markman, H. J. (2006). Sacrifice as a predictor of marital outcomes. *Family Process, 45*, 289–303.

Sternberg, R. J. (1986). A triangular theory of love. *Psychological Review, 93*, 119–135.

Sternberg, R. J. (1997). Construct validation of a triangular love scale. *European Journal of Social Psychology, 27*, 313–335.

Waldron, V. R., & Kelley, D. (2005). Forgiveness as a response to relational transgression. *Journal of Social and Personal Relationships, 22*, 723–742.

Waldron, V. R., & Kelley, D. L. (2008). *Communicating forgiveness.* Thousand Oaks, CA: Sage.

Worthington, E. L., Jr. (2006). *Forgiveness and reconciliation: Theory and application.* New York, NY: Routledge.

Worthington, E. L., Jr., & Drinkard, D. T. (2000). Promoting reconciliation through psychoeducational and therapeutic interventions. *Journal of Marital and Family Therapy, 26*, 93–101.

8

REIMAGINED RELATIONSHIPS

Community Applications and Lessons

He aha te mea I tea o? He tangata, he tangata, he tangata.
Translation: What is the most important thing in the world? People, people, people.
— Maori proverb

★

We believe that social science study that matters, that is transformative, should be conducted in ongoing dialogue with fellow citizens (Flyvbjerg, 2012, p. 25), firmly embedded in community. Doing so requires an iterative approach between theory, research, teaching, and practice. In this chapter, we describe what this experience has looked like for us, bringing (re)imagination to communities. We reflect on lessons learned in these communities. And we tell the story of how we have attempted to reimagine better relationships between researchers and non-academics – real people and real communities. We hope some of what we offer helps you do the same.

Doug and Vince have been researching and teaching about relationship reimagination most of their careers. The clearest example of this, their forgiveness work, spans two decades. Dayna joined the forgiveness project in 2006, first as a student and then as collaborator and colleague. Here we focus on forgiveness as one example of relationship imagination brought to various community settings.

During the early years, the audience for our work was mainly a captive one – the students in our courses on personal and work relationships, conflict management, and related topics. Thanks in large part to Doug's pioneering work, our academic colleagues soon started to express interest in the communication of forgiveness. That interest resulted in a series of conference presentations, journal articles (Kelley & Waldron, 2005; Waldron & Kelley, 2005), book chapters (Kelley & Waldron, 2006; Waldron, Kelley, & Harvey, 2008), and eventually, a book entitled *Communicating Forgiveness*. The book was a labor of love, but it was also a difficult collaboration among two friends with very different work styles and backgrounds. Vince and Doug joke that, in laboring to finish *Communicating Forgiveness*, they learned more about interpersonal forgiveness than they ever learned from the research!

Over time, interest in our work spread beyond the university and we started receiving invitations to speak about forgiveness with community groups. We shared our work with the local PBS affiliate, faith communities, parent–teacher organizations, senior centers, professional and civic organizations, and our university's branch of the Osher Lifelong Learning Institute, a vibrant learning community for older residents of the metropolitan Phoenix area. Without fail, members of these audiences were eager to learn about and talk about forgiveness. Most had internalized messages about the topic, having heard about its importance from parents, faith leaders, civil rights leaders, or mental health professionals. Some were aware that forgiveness had been incorporated somehow in well-known efforts to recover from ethnic violence, as in South Africa and Rwanda, nations that fashioned public processes of reconciliation to hold perpetrators accountable while creating possibilities for peaceful coexistence. But they wanted to know if university researchers had something to say specifically to them and their communities.

For years, we puzzled over the best ways to facilitate responsible discussions about forgiveness beyond the walls of the academy. The standard community presentation was fine, as far as it went, but we could devote only so much time to community service. And we knew it was the discussion that followed our "talking head" performances that generated the most energy in audiences and in us. Enter Dayna Kloeber, one of the authors of this book and a forgiveness scholar in her own right (see, for example, Kloeber, 2011; Kloeber & Waldron, 2017). In 2013, Dayna prototyped a facilitation process that came to be known as *The Forgiveness Tree Project* (FTP). The FTP uses discussion-based exercises and a simulated tree, including leaves, to help communities join together in a tangible expression of forgiveness ideals (e.g., empathy, compassion, dialogue). Table 8.1 provides a summary of the 17 sites and over 1,200 community members who have participated in Forgiveness Tree Ceremonies since the fall of 2013 (see Appendix A for a complete description of how to conduct a Forgiveness Tree Program).

These community experiences have helped shape our ideas in ways that make our theory and analysis more grounded. For example, audience members struggle, as we do still, with vexing questions about forgiveness, such as, "Is it ever 'right' to forgive a murderer or a child molester?" They wonder about the suffering that was created or experienced by their ancestors. What does it mean to seek forgiveness for slavery? The displacement or annihilation of indigenous peoples? The Holocaust? The abuse of children by Catholic clergy? Who has the right to seek and offer forgiveness in such cases? Some audience members respond more personally, quietly sharing their thoughts after the presentations. Many ponder personal questions. Can you forgive someone who "cheats" on you? What about

TABLE 8.1 Forgiveness Tree Ceremonies

Month/Year	Community	Audience	Attendees	Format			
				Community Speaker(s)	Breakout Sessions	Lecture	Discussion Circle(s)
September 2013	Sorority	Sorority members	100			✓	
March 2014	Northlight Art Gallery	Artists, curator, inmates' families, students	50	✓			✓
March 2014	Neighborhood Ministries Inner City Center	Staff, leaders	75			✓	
August 2014	Camp Solera	Freshman Residence Hall	300			✓	✓
October 2014	Glendale Community College/ Civility Week	Students, faculty	90				✓
November 2014	Adult Detention Center	Inmates, detention officers, graduate students	45	✓	✓		✓
April 2015	ASU's Consent Week	Abuse survivors	60	✓		✓	✓
April 2015	ASU's Family Communication Consortium Forgiveness Education Week	Undergraduate and graduate students	35			✓	✓

Month/Year	Community	Audience	Attendees	Format			
				Community Speaker(s)	Breakout Sessions	Lecture	Discussion Circle(s)
May 2015	Forgiveness Tree Donors Thank You Event	Donors, community FTP champions, students	60	✓		✓	
May 2015	Oakwood Elementary School	Middle school students, teachers, staff	220	✓	✓	✓	✓
August 2015	Arizona Boys' and Girls' Club	Staff training	40				✓
October 2015	Arizona Boys' and Girls' Club	Tweens and teens (12–18 yrs)	120			✓	✓
December 2015	Franciscan Renewal Center	Adult Staff (counselors, clergy, cooks, custodians)	50		✓	✓	✓
Fall 2016, Spring 2017	Arizona Boys' and Girls' Club Three Locations: A, B & C	Tweens (10–12 yrs), first and second graders	90			✓	✓
August 2017	Arizona State University Freshman Orientation Class	College Freshmen	15			✓	
Ongoing	Neighborhood Ministries Inner City Center	Children to adult, including staff	300	✓		✓	
Winter 2017	United Church of Christ & Unitarian Universalist Congregation	Adult congregation members	40	✓		✓	✓

an abusive uncle who apologizes or an absent father who reappears years later? Vince remembers a musclebound young man, back in school after a period of incarceration, who tearfully revealed his struggles to forgive himself for the shame he had caused his family. His comments, and many others, prompted us to reflect more deeply on the process of self-forgiveness.

Some audience members have been respectfully resistant, even angry. "But, why should I forgive the husband who walked out on me and my two kids?" asked one mom, voicing the very understandable frustration our topic sometimes surfaces. Short answer: *Maybe you shouldn't, at least not yet*. Still, others have shared their heartfelt efforts to forgive parents who disappointed, children who were ungrateful, spouses who proved unfaithful, and friends who pulled back when they should have stepped in to help. And some souls were clearly burdened by a pressure to forgive. Having been deeply hurt, they were distressed by a sense that they *should* forgive (and ideally "get over it"), a message often communicated by church, family, and even well-meaning friends. In the revelations of these anguished persons, doubly victimized as they were by an insensitive and uninformed rhetoric of forgiveness, we saw one of the dark sides of this potentially healing process. These forgiveness encounters with hurting people sobered us, but they also inspired us. Here was a topic that *really mattered* to people even when it was met with militant rejection. And even though we often had no answers, we realized that simply raising the right questions was a valuable service, one that allowed injured people and communities to voice their values, conflicted feelings, and the hope that they could reimagine their relationships and a future free of bitterness, alienation, and cycles of recrimination.

The Forgiveness Tree: An Exemplar of Reimagining Relationships

Before presenting our "lessons learned" from community engagement, it will be useful to overview the Forgiveness Tree Project and the diversity of community organizations with which we have partnered. Hopefully this will put some metaphorical "meat" (or maybe legumes, for our vegan friends) on our insights and stories as we describe the effects our community work has had on our thinking and practice.

Much of the social science work on forgiveness has been conducted by clinical psychologists who have championed forgiveness-based therapies. Our interest has primarily been located in how people in non-therapeutic relationships experience forgiveness and reconciliation. And all three of us have significant community involvements and have long been helping communities reimagine relationships in a variety of ways. Our academic pursuits and natural inclination toward community involvement came together when we heard research participants and students telling us that they were taught they *should* forgive, but seldom received instruction on *how* to do it. Practically, this often meant gritting teeth, stuffing emotions, and offering a simple, "Sorry", followed by, "It's okay. Forget it", instead of participating in a more complete healing and potentially reconciling process.

This prompted us to create a community intervention focused on imagination and discourse. Our communication-based approach to examining relationship disruption has most specifically focused on *behavior and meaning*. So what might a good (or lame) apology sound like? How do we know when it necessary to say the words "I forgive you?" In what ways can you assure a partner that your misdeed won't be repeated? What does it mean when someone offers conditional, rather than unconditional forgiveness ("I will forgive you but only if you do X")?

The *Forgiveness Tree Project* is discussion grounded; it invites participants to share their own understandings, experiences, and reservations about forgiveness. And it includes a ceremony in which audience members express their forgiveness understandings in written messages appended to a metaphorical "forgiveness tree". The tree provides individuals a way to take action, but is also an expression of the community's embrace of forgiveness as a shared value. (You will find a guide for conducting a forgiveness tree ceremony in Appendix A.)

Community Partners You'll Be Hearing About

In the following discussion we refer to various community organizations whose partnerships have been essential to our efforts. Previous intervention research indicates that key community individuals, known as program champions, are pivotal to successful implementation (Durlak & DuPre, 2008). Community champions are influential individuals in community organizations who are trusted by their staff and administrators, are able to rally support for new projects, and are highly invested in doing so (p. 337). By and large, community champions have *invited* us to conduct tree ceremonies in their communities. Here we profile a few.

Over the past five years, we have worked with various local Boys and Girls Clubs and grade schools. The degree to which the forgiveness tree ceremony has resonated with youthful audiences has been a joy. To date, these audiences have given us our only standing ovation. (Admittedly, middle-school students can be a little exuberant in crowds!) All teasing aside, some students' enthusiasm began in quiet, intimate moments. A six-year-old sat at her dad's office desk while he was watching the video we produced for the *Forgiveness Tree Project* (Kloeber, 2013). Asking if she could donate her own money, she told her dad, "We can show our love for others that need help in this world. I want to forgive my grandpa because he is not here with me right now because he made his choice to leave me and the rest of the family. But I will forgive him for [the] mistake he made and I still do love him." In fact, multiple children saw our video and asked if they could donate a small amount of allowance or babysitting money to the initial fundraising campaign. So when one of those young women approached Dayna about a year later and said she hoped to teach her middle-school friends about forgiveness, Dayna said, "Yes!" Together, they planned five springtime lunches filled with 12 student leaders, pizza, five loosely structured talks about forgiveness, tons of energy, plenty of sarcasm, and jokes Dayna did not always "get". In a variation of the train-the-trainer approach, the 12 student leaders then each recruited a friend to teach and help them prepare for the middle-school ceremony. Ultimately, the student leaders, Dayna, and a group of adult helpers led a group of approximately 200 seventh and eighth grade students in a forgiveness tree ceremony.

Our team has also been involved in numerous faith communities. One of our earliest invitations to conduct a train-the-trainer forgiveness tree session was at an inner-city neighborhood center where Doug has spent more than a decade nurturing relationships. Their 12-foot tall, 3D forgiveness tree, created by a local artist, still stands. Staff at the Franciscan Renewal Center invited us to help explore the role of forgiveness in their individual lives, in their relationships with each other, and with those who used the community's services. Nearly every staff member, including priests and spiritual educators, accountants, cooks, and janitors, participated in a half-day retreat guided by our team and facilitated by local leaders. Vince was also approached by the leadership of a local United Church of Christ congregation. After conversations with the minister, the community embedded discussions of forgiveness in the Sunday services of the Lenten season. Starting with the children, the congregants constructed and decorated a symbolic forgiveness tree, adding leaves with personal messages after each Sunday service. The minister integrated forgiveness into his sermons and the congregation's educational committee sponsored two film discussion nights, inviting community members and congregants to view segments of the documentary, *The Power of Forgiveness*.

Finally, we have conducted Forgiveness Tree Ceremonies for a variety of university organizations, including a residence hall, various freshman orientations, a sorority, and a consent group. The dean of students who coordinated the college freshman orientation envisioned teaching incoming students that forgiveness can be a positive conflict transformation strategy – highlighting various forgiveness components as shared community values especially useful to new students as they transition to living and working full-time among their peers.

Lessons Learned

In the following sections we reflect on our experience with our community partners. In these ponderings we highlight lessons learned regarding relationship imagination. We often use the *Forgiveness Tree Project* as an exemplar of employing a reimagination approach to relationship change, but we draw freely from other community examples, as well.

Lessons Learned From Ten–Year-Olds (and Grandparents): A Lifespan Perspective

> *Mercy means to hold someone on the ground until they beg you to let them up*
> – 10 year old boy from Boys and Girls Club

Over the years the Forgiveness Tree Program has been shared with preteens, teenagers, college students, parents, multi-aged adults, and elders. In approaching these diverse audiences, we are mindful of developmental differences. Forgiveness scholar Robert Enright and his colleagues (e.g., Enright & Fitzgibbons, 2015) have pioneered forgiveness education for children, describing a developmental sequence that progresses from a basic understanding of interpersonal conflict (some behaviors hurt other people), to an understanding of forgiveness as one possible response to conflict, to developing behaviors that are forgiving, and ultimately to an internalization of forgiveness as a personal virtue. We adapt the Forgiveness Tree Program to the age of the children we work with. For example, we adjust the kinds of "offenses" we discuss to be age-appropriate and our discussion of apologies is highly simplified for our younger participants. The roles played by children vary, too. Older children may be invited to serve as peer discussion facilitators or guides. Younger children participate by listening to stories, drawing, and adding "leaves" to the forgiveness tree. Following Enright and Fitzgibbons (2015), we have created forgiveness narratives to make our material engaging to children.

The quote that opens this section represents some of our work with ten-year-olds at the Boys and Girls Club. It came as a surprise to us that many ten-year-olds didn't know the meaning of the word *mercy*. In fact, one student actually confused mercy with revenge. This encouraged us to revisit the importance of mercy in understanding forgiveness. Do we define mercy for students, or do we work with terminology that is more readily a part of their experience, like kindness or generosity?

Outside the Boy and Girls Club we realized that adults, too, may struggle with the idea of mercy because it seems to let perpetrators "off the hook". With older audiences we offer less instruction and create more opportunities for individual sharing of forgiveness narratives – a recognition that life experience yields insight that can be useful to others. For instance, engaging a rich discussion as to whether mercy means there are no relational consequences to one's actions. Midlife is an especially important time to consider relationship reimagination, as it brings with it unique forms of adversity that may call for forgiveness and rethinking one's future, such as frayed relationships with adult children and aging parents or the relational consequences of a spouse's long-term abuse of substances such as alcohol (Waldron, 2017). Older audience members may be imagining forgiveness as they approach end of life, with limited time to heal damaged relationships and make amends.

Lessons Learned From Religious and Secular Audiences: So, a Rabbi, a Buddhist Priest, a Pastor, President of a Local Mosque's Congregation, and a Secular Humanist All Walk Into a Classroom

Forgiveness is Giving Someone the Opportunity to Change

This opening quote is from a rabbi who was invited to participate on a forgiveness panel in Doug's class – *Forgiveness, Mindfulness, and the Healthy Self*. It is simple and elegant. It taps into one of the key themes discussed previously in this text – reimagining our relationships is about rehumanizing the other. As we discussed previously, recognizing one's ability to change, to adapt, is central to treating one another as truly human (Oelofsen, 2009). Insights like this emerged from many of our conversations in faith communities.

As we noted earlier in this manuscript, we have been interested in religious contexts partly because religions tend to look at forgiveness as relational, and very much related to reconciliation. But, our interest is also much more personal. Doug came to the study of forgiveness from a contemplative Christian perspective. His academic work is in part an expression of central themes of his faith, including forgiveness, compassion, presence, and social justice. Vince, as a Unitarian Universalist, is part of a faith community that seeks wisdom from all religious faiths but also values science, art, and philosophy among its sources of inspiration. For him, forgiveness is an expression of a core commitment of this tradition – respecting the dignity of all people, no matter how flawed we may be. Vince's work on forgiveness is an extension of his research on the resilience of human relationships. Prior to her social scientific understanding of forgiveness, Dayna was guided by a lay perspective largely influenced by religion, literature, observation, and personal experience. She believes that people with less social, economic, health, and structural power have a complicated relationship with reconciliation and forgiveness. This belief drives her to conduct highly contextualized research on topics that include compassion, forgiveness, and resilience.

We often reveal our own religious and secular commitments in our work with community audiences. In this way, we are all intentional about recognizing the importance of religion in shaping the outlooks of so many of our audience members. We recognize that religious commitments can inspire people to be forgiving. When conducting a Forgiveness Tree Ceremony at a local, faith-based, inner-city nonprofit, a woman entered the room during the ceremony and began crying, then suddenly fell to the floor. Members of the community quickly came around her, prayed with her, and then guided her outside where two leaders were able to help her further. As we resumed the Forgiveness Tree Program ceremony, we all experienced a deep sense of our shared humanity and frailty. Our collective brokenness and need for forgiveness permeated the end of the ceremony as community members placed leaves on the forgiveness tree, representing their need to forgive, be forgiven, or embrace other aspects of reimagining our joint humanity and future.

We also know that religion can be a source of the pain, guilt, and pressure that make forgiveness and reconciliation problematic for some people. Working with community groups has made more evident our need to take into account that some people's resistance to forgive or reconcile comes from deep-seated religious beliefs or trauma. Recently Doug has been involved in an effort to put a "face" on immigration for certain church communities that have been polarized in the aftermath of recent political events. *Neighbor's Table* is a program that invites church members into immigrant family homes to share a meal and hear immigrants' stories. This process has helped humanize undocumented immigrants in the eyes of many church members as they imagine the plight and uncertain future of these families.

Lessons From Boys and Girls Club Staff: Forgiveness as Character Strength

> *When you seek revenge, you end up hurting the other person more than they hurt you . . . and then retaliation starts*
>
> – Hamara, Boys and Girls Club Member, Age 11

In our own scholarship, we define forgiveness as a process that surfaces, challenges, and affirms the moral commitments that guide us in our relationships (Waldron & Kelley, 2018). Since ancient times, philosophers have debated the degree to which forgiveness is rightly conceived as a moral obligation of the good person (see Griswold, 2007). The three of us are not in perfect agreement on this question, but we do agree that, compared to alienation, sustained bitterness, or revenge, it is preferable to reimagine our partnerships in ways that relieve human suffering and create possibilities for peaceful human relations.

In this sense, forgiveness can play a vital role in character education programs (e.g., Lin, Enright, & Klatt, 2011), as well as those that focus on good relationships. Early meetings with Boys and Girls Club staff regarding implementation of the Forgiveness Tree Program in their clubs quickly framed this aspect of forgiveness work as character strength. Staff members are clear about the fact that they are not simply providing a place for kids to "hang out" after school. They place a high priority on the character and leadership development of their students. As one site manager reported during a debrief of the Forgiveness Tree Program, "I've never seen anything like this at the Boys & Girls Club. You are teaching the kids important things they might not otherwise learn in their lives. Forgiveness is something that the kids need to learn to help them in their relationships."

Lessons Learned From Intact Communities: Claiming Who We Are

Traits of forgiveness, like compassion and empathy and safe relationships, are the very values upon which we hope to build our community

Due to the good work of clinical psychologists, forgiveness is often conceptualized as an individual decision, which, of course, it is. But the Forgiveness Tree Project assumes that forgiveness occurs within the context of larger social collectives, such as families, schools, and communities. We build on the work of others who have offered forgiveness education in at-risk communities burdened by poverty and a history of intergroup conflict (Gassin, Enright, & Knutson, 2005). Our facilitations often are attended by multiple members of communities, and ideally, the whole community is represented. In fact, one of the metaphorical goals of the forgiveness tree metaphor is to grow a "whole forest" of forgiveness, not just a single tree. The ceremonial component of the Forgiveness Tree Project is the communal construction of a tree that is as an expression and enduring symbol of the group's willingness to practice forgiveness. For this idea to take hold, we seek buy-in from community leaders (champions) and we may cultivate key members to be forgiveness advocates through a "train-the-trainer" effort that spans several sessions prior to the community gathering. Although we can claim only limited success thus far, our intent is to leave a group with the skills, leadership com-mitments, and the ongoing support required to truly become a more forgiving community.

As the opening statement represents, many communities embrace the essential values embodied in an imaginative forgiveness process. In this particular case (during new student orientation), however, we knew that we were fighting an uphill battle in many regards. For instance, this seminar was held during orientation at the beginning of the school year when many people are focused on the future, trying to enjoy the present, not working on the past. In addition, we knew that not all incoming students would think they had forgiveness issues to work on or be ready to work on the ones they had. As such, we reexamined our work, kneading the concepts and models until central themes related to incoming first-year students shook out. The result was a marvelous day focusing on dialogue, empathy, release, justice, promise, and courage. Hopefully we helped lay a foundation for healing the hurt and conflicts, to come, in these students' first year at university.

Lessons Learned Through Embracing Culture and Imagination

My dad told me if he ever learned that I walked away from a fight, he would kick my ass
— Adolescent boy from Boys and Girls Club

We must not think evil of this man
— Quotation of an Amish elder participant from Paul (2012)

Forgiveness education must be grounded in its cultural context, as the contrast of the above quotations exemplifies. Its value relative to other responses, such as revenge, varies across communities. Both opening quotations demonstrate deep underlying cultural values. The first is from a young man who grew up in a culture that highly valued a version of masculinity deeply rooted in saving face through fighting and aggression. To teach forgiveness without taking this into account would be careless, if not irresponsible. By contrast, the second quotation is from Paul (2012) who examined Amish culture to better understand the deeply held preference of forgiveness as a response to even the most heinous forms of wrongdoing. In our own work with children from a community marred by gang conflict and cultural tension, we found that some parents thought it necessary to prepare their children to respond to threats with physical measures. It was against this cultural backdrop that we taught children forgiveness as an alternative response. To ground our approach in the cultural experiences of children we have taken such steps as listening to the narratives they share about relational conflicts, encouraging them to reflect on the value of forgiveness in their families and neighborhoods, and crafting instructional narratives that reflect their circumstances.

Our efforts to create an intervention that is culturally sensitive have been partially guided by work from colleagues such as Colby et al. (2013) and Pettigrew and Hecht (2015) who do work with adolescent substance abuse prevention. We have also taken inspiration from successful intervention teams such as the University of Queensland, who began an intervention over 40 years ago called The Triple P-Positive Parenting Program (Sanders, Markie-Dadds, & Turner, 2003). Their model has stood the test of time by being strongly theoretical, scientific, creatively disseminated, and highly culturally contextual.

All of this came crashing home for Doug during a Forgiveness Tree Program at one of our local jails. During a discussion period with male inmates, Doug had mentioned that his mother and father had divorced when he was seven and that he had primarily grown up with his mom. After the ceremony an inmate walked up to him and, with tears in his eyes, asked, "How did you turn out okay without a dad?" Doug was stunned. Such commonality embedded in the midst of apparent cultural difference. Before Doug could respond, a prison guard came and escorted the inmates away. This experience reminded us all of our shared humanity, and the importance of taking into account the deep cultural experiences that uniquely shape us.

Lessons Learned From Boys and Girls Clubs: Safety, Apology, and Going With the Flow

I said, "Sorry – Trollnose!"

– Martin, middleschool student

As it turns out, adolescents have a lot to say about forgiveness. Boys and Girls Club students have brought local, highly contextualized experiences to our program about forgiveness and reimagining relationships: gaming conflicts, exclusion from social invitations, and the foibles of young romance are just a few of the painful topics they explore. Working closely with staff, we learned that a survey of youth at the clubs revealed preteens want to develop improved skills for managing peer conflict. We adapted the Forgiveness Tree Program to help these youth learn that forgiveness can be a strong response to hurtful behavior, one that cultivates respect while preserving valued relationships. As we pilot-tested the program at three community sites we quickly realized we would have to adapt to this challenging environment. A young woman's query, as to if she could forgive someone for stabbing her, was a poignant reminder of the importance of what we do and the need to understand the difference between forgiveness and reconciliation. Questions like this were the impetus for emphasizing emotional, psychological, and physical safety when forgiving or talking to adult third parties.

Our involvement with Boys and Girls Clubs also put a renewed emphasis on how we think about and teach apology. Preliminary results of a Boys and Girls Clubs pilot study indicated that teaching children how to apologize is especially important, as well as teaching them how to communicate with adults (teachers, parents, administrators) who "force" them to apologize (Kloeber, Hanna, Becker, & Razzante, 2017). Feeling especially indignant at being forced by a playground aide to apologize to a fellow student, one young man (the author of our opening quote in this section) reported he had angrily exclaimed to the other student, "I said, 'Sorry – Trollnose!'" Our weekly sessions provided time to work through many scenarios children could recall. One way we tackled this issue was by creating a playful activity that encouraged students to imagine the worst way they could apologize (we had great fun with this!), followed by creating a more effective, appropriate apology.

In terms of working with children and nonprofits, a consistent lesson has been to *go with the flow*. Kids are an energetic, wildly funny, and sometimes unpredictable bunch. During one exercise that involved writing on pieces of toilet paper, the kids were so keyed up that one of our leaders consented to letting them cover her with toilet paper, just to release some energy. She looked like our "forgiveness mummy". Other times, even after calling staff the day before to confirm date and time of our workshop, we arrived to find the students scattered, or one time, gone on a field trip. Going with the flow was a good reminder to us that working with all people is an exercise in imagination, forgiveness, and reconciliation.

BOX 8.1 WHAT CHILDREN HAVE TO TEACH US

Working with children has taught us a tremendous amount about our own theorizing and research. Having to break our forgiveness model down to fit into four one-hour sessions, appropriate to 10-year-olds, helped us reconsider the essential components of what we study. That being said, we strongly hope that other impassioned researchers will embark on the opportunity to teach kids. Whether it be forgiveness, nonviolence techniques, or connecting skills like listening, we have a lot to learn from children and youth, and we think they have a lot to learn from us. Unique insights from minors are sadly underrepresented in communication scholarship (Miller-Day, Pezalla, & Chesnut, 2013), as many scholars are intimidated by the Internal Review Board protocols for this protected population. Fortunately, pedagogical models set forth by scholars such as Clark (2015) and Pettigrew, Miller-Day, Krieger, and Hecht (2011) can help.

Lessons Learned in Prisons and Art Galleries: Reimagining Self and Other

Our Forgiveness Tree team has also learned from family members of incarcerated adults, a detention officer from an adult detention center, and an artist (Jane) whose life's passion was to teach incarcerated adults to use art as a productive outlet for their anger, grief, guilt, shame, and sorrow. An on-campus art gallery, who had partnered with a local adult detention center for an art installation, invited us join in a night of reimagining self and other through art and a Forgiveness Tree Ceremony. The ambience and mood of this ceremony remains a favorite memory. The ceremony took place at night, in an intimate three-room art museum on campus. In our audience there were ASU students, professors, and faculty from across campuses and disciplines. Jane bravely explained that by channeling her energy into this artwork with the incarcerated, she was slowly able to work through the rage she harbored toward her daughter's violent rapist. At her lowest point, she admitted that she had purchased a gun and began learning how to use it, in preparation to unleash her rage on him once he was apprehended. She recounted that, during that dark time, she realized she needed to learn about forgiveness – that her own life depended on it. Jane, like so many others we have talked with, has felt the need to work toward forgiveness for her own well-being. Her story, her honesty, and her willingness to share are part of what continues to drive us toward bringing forgiveness education and Forgiveness Tree Ceremonies to communities. That spring evening was five years ago, and yet Dayna still vividly recalls the stillness in the room while Jane spoke, surrounded by inmates' artwork that hung on the walls and was suspended from the ceilings.

Later that year, our team took a group of graduate students to the adult detention center that made the leaves for that memorable evening. We thanked them for the leaves they sent us, praised them for their artwork, and listened to what they had been learning about forgiveness from their detention officer. It was a stunning experience. Spread across one community room wall was the trunk of a tree, with interwoven branches, all created by an artist/inmate from available and recyclable materials – paper bags, fabric, remnants of cards, and other art projects. Their artistry in the roots of the tree contained words such as "poverty", "pain", "fear", and "fatherless". Most of the inmates read letters they had spent months drafting. A significant take-away for us was the profound sense of shame, especially from inmates who had children. Here they sat, unable to mother and father their children as they wanted. As communication scholars, our initial exploration of forgiveness was focused on relational, outward expressions. However, experiences like this changed the place we gave to self-forgiveness, a critical sense-making process essential to reimagining healthy futures.

Final Imaginations

We opened this chapter by explaining that social science that matters is in ongoing dialogue with fellow citizens (Flyvbjerg, 2012, p. 25). This is an iterative process of tacking between theory, research, and praxis. A fellow scholar, in his work with homeless populations and compassion, calls this process "presence" – being with people to better understand their experience (Huffman, 2017). Doug facilitates students' presence in his inner-city families service learning course – no exams, just hang out with urban youth, and let their *presence* change you. This is the heart of our community experiences – presence, dialogue, transformation. To our team, and to all of our courageous community partners communities, a special thanks as you have inspired us to reimagine the way we think about ourselves and our relationships.

References

Clark, L. E. (2015). *Grieving adolescents co-perform collective compassion in a concert of emotions as they stop! In the name of love at Comfort Zone Camp.* Tempe: Arizona State University.

Colby, M., Hecht, M. L., Miller-Day, M., Krieger, J. L., Syvertsen, A. K., Graham, J. W., & Pettigrew, J. (2013). Adapting school-based substance use prevention curriculum through cultural grounding: A review and exemplar of adaptation processes for rural schools. *American Journal of Community Psychology, 51*, 190–205. doi:10.1007/s10464-012-9524-8

Durlak, J. A., & DuPre, E. P. (2008). Implementation matters: A review of research on the influence of implementation on program outcomes and the factors affecting implementation. *American Journal of Community Psychology, 41*(3–4), 327–350. doi:10.1007/s10464-008-9165-0

Enright, R. D., & Fitzgibbons, R. P. (2015). *Forgiveness therapy: An empirical guide to resolving anger and restoring hope.* Washington, DC: American Psychological Association.

Flyvbjerg, B. (2012). Making social science matter. In G. Papanagnou (Ed.), *Social science and policy challenges: Democracy, values, and capacities* (pp. 25–56). Paris, France: Unesco Publishing.

Gassin, E. A., Enright, R. D., & Knutson, J. A. (2005). Bringing peace to the central city: Forgiveness education in Milwaukee. *Theory Into Practice, 44*(4), 319–328. doi:10.1207/s15430421tip4404_5

Griswold, C. L. (2007). Plato and forgiveness. *Ancient Philosophy, 27*(2), 269–287. doi:10.5840/ancientphil20072723

Huffman, T. P. (2017). Compassionate communication, embodied aboutness, and homeless young adults. *Western Journal of Communication, 81*(2), 149–167.

Kelley, D. L., & Waldron, V. R. (2005). An investigation of forgiveness-seeking communication and relational outcomes. *Communication Quarterly, 53*, 339–358.

Kelley, D. L., & Waldron, V. R. (2006). Forgiveness: Communicative implications in social relationships. In C. Beck (Ed.), *Communication Yearbook 30* (pp. 303–342). Mahwah, NJ: Lawrence Erlbaum.

Kloeber, D. (Producer). (2013, December 5). *The forgiveness tree project* [YouTubeVideo]. Retrieved from https://youtube.com/watch?v=WflGyKojGd8

Kloeber, D. N. (2011). Voicing conditional forgiveness. Tempe: Arizona State University.

Kloeber, D. N., Hanna K. N., Becker, C. J., & Razzante, R. J. (2017). *A qualitative analysis of the forgiveness tree curriculum at boys and girls club: Methods, results, and recommendations* (unpublished). Internal Arizona State University, Tempe.

Kloeber, D. N., & Waldron, V. R. (2017). Expressing and suppressing conditional forgiveness in serious romantic relationships. In J. A. Samp (Ed.), *Communicating interpersonal conflict in close relationships: Contexts, challenges, and opportunities* (pp. 250–266). New York, NY: Routledge.

Lin, W. N., Enright, R., & Klatt, J. (2011). Forgiveness as character education for children and adolescents. *Journal of Moral Education, 40*(2), 237–253. doi:10.1080/03057240.2011.568106

Miller-Day, M., Pezalla, A., & Chesnut, R. (2013). Children are in families too! The presence of children in communication research. *Journal of Family Communication, 13*(2), 150–165.

Oelofsen, R. (2009). De-and rehumanization in the wake of atrocities. *South African Journal of Philosophy/Suid-Afrikaanse Tydskrif vir Wysbegeerte, 28*(2), 178–188.

Paul, G. D. (2012). "We must not think evil of this man": A case study of Amish and English forgiveness. *Communication Quarterly, 60*(3), 424–444. doi:10.1080/01463373.2012.688722

Pettigrew, J., & Hecht, M. L. (2015). Developing school-based prevention curricula. In K. Bosworth (Ed.), *Prevention science in school settings* (pp. 151–174). New York, NY: Springer.

Pettigrew, J., Miller-Day, M., Krieger, J., & Hecht, M. L. (2011). Alcohol and other drug resistance strategies employed by rural adolescents. *Journal of Applied Communication Research, 39*(2), 103–122.

Sanders, M. R., Cann, W., & Markie_Dadds, C. (2003). The triple P_Positive parenting programme: A universal population_level approach to the prevention of child abuse. *Child Abuse Review, 12*(3), 155–171. doi:10.1002/car.798

Waldron, V. (2017). *Middle years of marriage: Challenge, change, and growth.* New York, NY: Peter Lang.

Waldron, V. R., & Kelley, D. (2005). Forgiveness as a response to relational transgression. *Journal of Social and Personal Relationships, 22*, 723–742.

Waldron, V. R., & Kelley, D. L. (2018). Negotiated morality theory: How family communication shapes our values. In D. O. Braithwaite, E. A. Suter, & K. Floyd (Eds.), *Engaging theories in family communication: Multiple perspectives* (2nd ed., pp. 233–243). New York, NY: Taylor & Francis.

Waldron, V., Kelley, D., & Harvey, J. (2008). Forgiving communication and relational consequences. In M. Motley (Ed.), *Studies in applied interpersonal communication* (pp. 165–184). Newbury Park, CA: Sage Publications.

APPENDIX A: INTERESTED IN CONDUCTING A FORGIVENESS TREE CEREMONY?

This appendix is designed to provide guidance for readers interested in conducting a Forgiveness Tree Ceremony. In the following pages, you will find outlines of learning objectives, photos of previous forgiveness trees, a list of supplies needed, and an outline of the forgiveness tree ceremony event, complete with curriculum detail. In this way, we hope to serve multiple styles of teaching and prepping. Nothing will make us happier than leaders who take what we have provided and make it their own. For additional information, including pictures from previous ceremonies, instructions, and additional resources, visit our website: http://forgivenesstree.weebly.com/.

What Does a Forgiveness Tree Look Like?

We are frequently asked, "What does a forgiveness tree look like?" And, it is not unusual for one of us to quickly pull out a cell phone to display photos. Figures A.1 to A.5 provide some examples.

Creating a Forgiveness Tree Ceremony

Learning Objectives

- Learn what forgiveness is and isn't.
- Learn why forgiveness is important in relationships and communities.
- Learn some basics about how to seek, grant, and receive forgiveness.
- Reflect on one's own forgiveness-related values and commitments.
- Explore what it means to be a forgiving community.

FIGURE A.1 Art Gallery

FIGURE A.2 Pinal County Detention Center

FIGURE A.3 ASU Freshman Orientation

FIGURE A.4 Consent Week, Arizona State University

FIGURE A.5 Faith-based Inner-City Neighborhood Center, Neighborhood Ministries

Art Supply Suggestions

- Brown paper for tree roots.
- Brown paper for tree trunk and branches.
- Green (or other colors) paper for tree leaves.
- Leaf pattern (recommended the community pre-cuts leaves).
- Adhesive for attaching paper to the wall (pre-test on your wall surface).
- Alternative: Pre-cut trees and leaves are often available through teaching supply stores and websites.

Curriculum Notes

- Introduction.
- What forgiveness is and isn't.
- Why forgiveness is important.
- Communication of forgiveness.
- Transitions between (a) intro and education, (b) education and leaf-writing, (c) leaf-writing and attaching leaves, (d) attaching leaves and closing the ceremony.
- Conclusion.

Event Outline

Although each audience and ceremony has a distinct culture, and unique lessons to learn, in our five years of conducting Forgiveness Tree Ceremonies in 17 communities with over 1,200 people we have discovered that the following agenda works well. The times listed are approximate for a 75–90-minute ceremony and can be adjusted based on the audience and occasion. We have often modified this structure for half-day or multiple-week sessions that culminate with the ceremony.

- Part I: Community champion introduces forgiveness tree celebrant (2–3 minutes).
- Part II: Forgiveness tree celebrant speaks (5–6 minutes).
- Part III: Forgiveness education/discussion (20–40 minutes, as time and audience allow).
- Part IV: Leaf-writing/self-reflection by audience (5–7 minutes).
- Part V: Attachment of leaves to the tree by audience (10 minutes).
- Part VI: Closing remarks by celebrant (5 minutes).
- Take photos!!

Barking Up the Right (Forgiveness) Tree: Details and Lessons Learned

In this section, we do our best to take some of what we have learned from the Forgiveness Tree Ceremonies we have conducted, and the trees other communities have planted, to help you envision and plan parts I–VI.

Community Champion Introduces Forgiveness Tree Celebrant (2–3 Minutes)

We recommend that a community champion (Durlak & DuPre, 2008) make the initial introduction. Usually this is a person in the community who reached out to us, having noticed a need for forgiveness education in their community. Our community champions have ranged in age from 13 to 60+ years of age and have held a variety of leadership positions in their organizations. Some examples include: President of a student organization, managing director of youth center, art studio director, detention officer, dean of students, residence hall director, renewal center director, church lay leader, director of an inner-city faith-based neighborhood center, and many others. Their introductions have ranged from extemporaneous and informal to more structured and ceremonial, depending on their preferences. The champion has intimate knowledge of the community's culture and generally has a feel for how forgiveness resonates with the audience. *We cannot stress enough how much we consider this person to be the cultural expert in their community.* We encourage the champion to make a brief, two-minute introduction, but some especially passionate champions have asked for more time. Alternately, some champions prefer to quickly turn over the program to the forgiveness tree ceremony celebrant (the individual who will be guiding the *Forgiveness Tree* ceremony).

Celebrant Message

The celebrant should be a person is who is very familiar with the forgiveness tree curriculum and has public speaking experience. The primary aims of the celebrant's message are to (a) get the audience's attention, (b) introduce the relevance and significance of forgiveness, (c) explain that together they will be "planting their community's forgiveness tree", and (d) preview the agenda segments toward that end. To get the audience's attention and to introduce the relevance and significance of forgiveness, a brief personal narrative from a community member is especially powerful.

Often a strong beginning is rather straightforward: "Today, we are going to plant the Arizona State University Forgiveness Tree." With kids' ceremonies, Dayna and other leaders have had success by playfully asking, "Who wants to plant the Boys and Girls Club Forgiveness Tree?" But again, we cannot stress enough how important it is to match the mood of this introduction to the culture of the group. Dayna's forgiveness tree ceremony with the consent group was a much more quiet, somber event.

Forgiveness Education/Discussion

The education portion consists of the following segments: (1) what forgiveness is and isn't and why it is important, (2) communicating forgiveness, and (3) the forgiveness tree metaphor. The length of the forgiveness education portion depends on the audience. Dayna facilitated a simple scaled-down version with a group of incoming college freshmen as part of an orientation course that lasted about 15–20 minutes. Typical ceremonies have been a total of about 90 minutes, in which case the education section is around 45 minutes. However, we have conducted much longer sessions – the Franciscan Renewal Center session was scheduled for five hours. We have also presented a longer forgiveness education curriculum to youth, both at a local middle school and at Boys and Girls Clubs. This consisted of four modules lasting for about 75 minutes each, culminating in a 60–90-minute tree ceremony. In these ceremonies youth were trained over multiple modules to help facilitate the forgiveness tree experience with younger students. Below is an outline of the sections named above.

What Forgiveness Is/Isn't and Why It Is Important

- It is an acknowledgment of wrongdoing by you or someone else.
- It is an openness to deeper understanding of the offender and his or her circumstances and experiences.
- It is a commitment to hold yourself and others accountable to cherished individual and community values.
- It is a decision to forgo your (understandable) desire for recrimination, grudge-holding, or revenge.
- It is an effort to transform your feelings, thoughts, and behavior toward the offender from negative to positive (or at least neutral or less negative).
- It is commonly a blend of negative and positive affect, emotion, and communication.
- It is not excusing or condoning bad behavior.
- It is not minimizing bad behavior.
- It is not denying bad behavior.
- It is not reconciliation.
- It is associated with mental and physical health benefits.

Communicating Forgiveness (Waldron & Kelley, 2008)

- Acknowledging wrongdoing.
- Making sense of transgressions.

- Expressing emotion.
- Seeking forgiveness.
- Granting forgiveness.
- Renegotiating shared relational moral values.
- Negotiating reconciliation in safe relationships.

The Forgiveness Tree Metaphor

The metaphor will resonate differently with each audience. We wholeheartedly agree with Lakoff and Johnson (1980/2003) when they explain that, "Meaning is not cut and dried; it is a matter of imagination" (p. 227). By this point in the book, you know we believe in not just imagination – but reimagination. We hope you and your audiences will make metaphorical connections that have not yet occurred to us. One group that Doug worked with added fruit to the tree, to represent the lasting outcomes of forgiveness in their community. Nevertheless, below is a guide to inspire some thought:

- Roots: Forgiveness-related values – personal, religious, cultural.
- Trunk: Healthy self.
- Branches: Relationships.
- Leaves: Renewal, redemption, healing.

Roots are the values, or what some have called root rules. These can be values about forgiveness and standards, principles, and ideals that characterize the community itself. For example, communities may value nonviolence, honesty, trust, emotional connection, mercy, and physical, emotional, and psychological safety. We emphasize that a healthy root system is maintained by a nourishing environment and continues to grow throughout the lifespan of the tree. We focus on the roots as the *community's shared values* and emphasize that the *Forgiveness Tree* ceremony is more than just working through each individual's problems.

The trunk symbolizes the healthy self which supports the rest of the tree. It can be represented by statements such as, "I cannot control what others say and do, but I can make choices about what I say and do". We often highlight elements about tree trunks, such as, if the roots are healthy (our personal and shared values), the trunk is healthy, but if the roots are somehow compromised, the trunk will likely show signs of this. The trunk supports the weight of the branches (our relationships). If our relationships are to be healthy, *we have to make healthy choices as individuals.*

The branches symbolize our relationships: Family, friends, colleagues, classmates, teammates, and neighbors, and we would argue even our foes. Some of the branches are so tightly connected to the trunk that losing them would drastically alter the tree. This can be the case when relationships end, either due to external factors such as moving or physical death, or because of decisions we make after experiencing relational disappointment, hurt, and pain. Sometimes branches need a little pruning to preserve the overall health of the tree. To do this it may be wise to hire an arborist, or in people's case – a therapist, counselor, clergy, support group, or a close friend or family member. And sometimes, as most of us probably know, it may just be necessary to discontinue a relationship with someone, or at the very least, adjust our boundaries in a significant way. Fortunately, just like with trees, frequent and consistent pruning, nurturing, and fertilizing makes the need for major pruning much less likely.

The leaves symbolize relationship growth and renewal, a process encouraged by the communication of forgiveness. Spring leaves are evidence of hope and resilience and they signal recovery from the trying times of winter or drought. When participants create and inscribe leaves, they express what they have learned about forgiveness, including new understandings, skills, and motivations that may help them renew their connections with others. The messages of renewal sometimes concern self-forgiveness and the revitalization of spirit that accompanies it. Some leaves express the participants' desires for a more forgiving community. Often, during the tree ceremony, we refocus participants' thoughts on the communicative aspects of forgiveness. Sincerity, truth-telling, apologies, acknowledging and validating emotion, making amends, apology, asking for forgiveness, saying "I forgive you" – all of these messages are what we do to create forgiveness in our personal relationships and communities (Waldron & Kelley, 2008). It's how we do forgiveness. It's how we talk forgiveness into being.

As the education section draws to an end, the celebrant begins to transition to the leaf-writing section of the ceremony.

Self-Reflection and Leaf-Writing

Participants write forgiveness messages on leaves during this segment, which usually takes 5–7 minutes. Leaves are usually fashioned from paper, but can be made from other handy materials. The communities have used colored copy paper, construction paper, tissue paper, pre-cut leaf-shaped Post-It notes (available online), and other decorative papers, to name a few. The jail used recycled materials such as paper lunch bags, fabric, cards, and yarn. The leaves, pens, and tape (or other adhesive) should all be on the tables prior to the start of the ceremony. Community participants have written a variety of forgiveness messages on leaves. Some have written things that were memorable to them from the education segment. Some examples include: "Forgiving is not forgetting", "Forgiveness takes time", and "Tatience" (combination of time and patience). Some bright incoming freshman recently wrote on their leaves, "I learned that it is important to voice forgiveness" and "I would like to learn how to forgive myself to make my relationships stronger".

Figures A.6 to A.8 show some examples.

FIGURE A.6

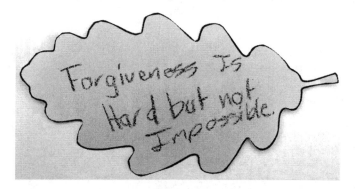

FIGURE A.7

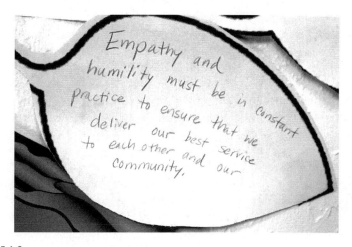

FIGURE A.8

Community Ceremony

As people finish writing their leaves (many people write on multiple leaves), the celebrant encourages audience members to attach their leaves to the tree. We have noticed that this portion of the ceremony usually takes on a communal feeling; we almost always write leaves too. Some people want to quietly attach their leaves whereas others want to visit and share. The length of this segment is largely determined by the size of the group. For example, 250+ college freshmen took about 15 minutes to attach leaves. After everyone has attached leaves, it is time to close the ceremony.

Forgiveness Tree as an Enduring Community Symbol

With everyone seated again, naming (or proclaiming) the community's forgiveness tree is the next important element. For example, "Boys and Girls Club Forgiveness Tree" or "Neighborhood Ministry's Forgiveness Tree". Finally, we make some type of statement to remind people of the significance of the overall process, something like: "This forgiveness tree is an enduring symbol of the community's commitment to consider forgiveness as an alternative to bitterness, anger and revenge." In some communities the tree remains displayed in a central location for some time. At the United Church of Christ church, the tree stood through the Lenten season, with members adding leaves to the tree each Sunday.

Other Helpful Information We Have Learned

Engaging the Community Early in the Planning Process

As previously discussed, the community forgiveness champion is usually the contact and is a powerful conduit for planning the event. During the planning stages with the community champion, we aim to (a) gain insight about the community through attentive listening or visiting the site, (b) jointly coordinate the event, and (c) encourage the champion to assemble the forgiveness tree roots, trunk, branches, and leaf preparation. Typically, through the planning stages, via e-mail, text, telephone, and usually a combination of all three, the champion shares their cultural expertise with one or more members of our team.

Inspiring the Individual Aesthetic of Each Tree

We encourage the community champion to be involved in planning the individual aesthetic of their tree and to prepare leaves in the week(s) and/or days leading up to the ceremony. We have seen this take a variety of forms. Inmates made leaves from colored copy paper for a forgiveness ceremony attended by their family members at a local art studio. Middle-school students created a site committee who communicated with faculty and staff to create a feature wall in their school's auditorium that remained displayed from late spring through eighth grade promotion. They also created a tree crafting committee. They used twisted brown butcher paper to create three-dimensional roots, trunk, and branches of the tree and created leaves from colored construction paper, using bright silk flowers to embellish their tree. A graduate student created a beautiful tree made from burlap, yarn, and paper and mounted it on a piece of cloth that was then suspended by rope in a local art studio that had an urban flare. Some have preferred to use premade trees from a teacher's supply store. The church engaged the services of a local artist, who created the outline of a large tree that was displayed in the sanctuary.

Some communities have used their tree preparation time to talk about forgiveness while they are crafting the tree roots, trunks, branches and leaves. Inmates at the adult detention center spent a month talking about forgiveness with their detention officer, who was in touch with us periodically throughout that time. While together, they cut out leaves, talked about forgiveness, shared emotional vulnerability, and wrote essays and letters about what forgiveness meant to them. Those who chose to do so read their essays aloud during our visit.

Final Imaginings

We hope you will consider adopting, and adapting, this model as you endeavor to reimagine relationships in your own communities. The *Forgiveness Tree Project* is only one example of how imagination and creativity can be used to encourage communities and their members to strengthen and transform their deepest-held relational values. We encourage you to let us know how you adapt this model to engage your own communities as we all work together in *Reimagining Our Relationships*.

References

Durlak, J. A., & DuPre, E. P. (2008). Implementation matters: A review of research on the influence of implementation on program outcomes and the factors affecting implementation. *American Journal of Community Psychology, 41*(3–4), 327–350. doi:10.1007/s10464-008-9165-0

Lakoff, G., & Johnson, M. (Ed.). (2003). *Metaphors we live by*. Chicago, IL: The University of Chicago Press. (Original work published 1980)

Waldron, V. R., & Kelley, D. L. (2008). *Communicating forgiveness*. Thousand Oaks, CA: Sage.

INDEX